I0475226

Doing
Da Vinci
For Kids

Catherine McGrew Jaime

Other Non-Fiction Books by Catherine Jaime:
Da Vinci: His Life and His Legacy
In Art: Leonardo
Exploring Da Vinci's Last Supper
Leonardo da Vinci Topical Study

Historical Fiction by Catherine Jaime:
Leonardo the Florentine
Leonardo: Masterpieces in Milan
Leonardo: To Mantua and Beyond
Leonardo: A Return to Florence
Failure in Philadelphia?
The Attack Trilogy

Creative Learning Connection

8006 Old Madison Pike, Ste 11-A
Madison, Alabama 35758
U.S.A.
www.CreativeLearningConnection.com

Copyright © Catherine McGrew Jaime, 2011, 2015

You may copy any portion of this book for use with your family or class, including, but not limited to the maps, charts, timeline, and overviews.

Pictures that are not in the public domain are used with permission from Dover Coloring Books and Dover Clip Art.

TABLE OF CONTENTS

NOTE TO TEACHERS/PARENTS

A couple of precautionary thoughts if da Vinci is a new topic of study for you:

1. Leonardo da Vinci was accused anonymously of inappropriate behavior during his youth – the charges were dropped; there was no real proof, but some books and websites elaborate unnecessarily on the incident.

2. Leonardo studied human anatomy extensively, and countless numbers of his *drawings/ sketches* show that interest. You may want to pick the books and websites your students look at accordingly.[1] I also take the liberty of "clothing" Leonardo's famous "Vitruvian Man," because the principles he was illustrating are impressive, even if I don't find Leonardo's original drawing necessarily "kid-friendly."

---

[1] *I found very few books or websites that could be shared with my students without a fair amount of creative editing first.*

INTRODUCTION

"Study the science of art and the art of science." [2]

I have been teaching students about the amazing works of Leonardo da Vinci for many years. Students of all ages are intrigued by his varied interests and abilities.

This book can be used alone as an introduction to da Vinci, or in conjunction with the more in-depth book, *Da Vinci: His Life and His Legacy.* [3] It could be enjoyed by one or more students on their own, or as the basis for one or more classes on da Vinci. Several of the times I've taught da Vinci, we've done one of the topics here (scientist, artist, inventor) each week.

The topics are not arranged in as random an order as they appear – they correlate to different periods of his life – and are laid out in the same chronological order they appear in *Da Vinci: His Life and His Legacy*. I've

---

[2] *Unless otherwise noted, the quotes and the drawings scattered throughout the book are from Leonardo himself.*
[3] *There is a bit of overlap between the two books, but very little. (For instance, the two maps appear in both, as does my slightly edited Vitruvian man and the corresponding chart.)*

included a one page overview of each of the periods of his life, so you have a context for them. You may, of course, study/teach the topics in any order you prefer.

Most of us think of art when we think of Leonardo da Vinci; in fact our minds usually go straight to the Mona Lisa or the Last Supper. But da Vinci did so much more than just art. He was an engineer, an inventor, an architect, a mathematician...The list goes on. He was the true "Renaissance man."

One of the many times da Vinci was ready for a change of pace in his life, he wrote a very unusual "job application letter" to the Duke of Milan. In that letter he described to the Duke the various types of things that he could do for the Duke. We will come back to different portions of that letter throughout our study. For older students, reading and analyzing this letter can be a great introduction to Leonardo da Vinci.

The map of Italy that follows the letter shows the places in Italy that Leonardo lived or visited for an extended period of time. (Italy was not a country yet, and many of the cities shown were independent city-states at the time.) And the map of Europe shows several other important da Vinci related locations.

To My Lord the Duke of Milan,
Florence, 1482

Most Illustrious Lord,

Having until now sufficiently considered the specimens of all those who proclaim themselves skilled contrivers of instruments of war, and that the invention and operation of the said instruments are nothing different to those in common use:

I shall endeavor, without prejudice to any one else, to explain myself to your Excellency showing your Lordship my secrets, and then offering them to your best pleasure and approbation to work with effect at opportune moments as well as all those things which in part, shall be briefly noted below:

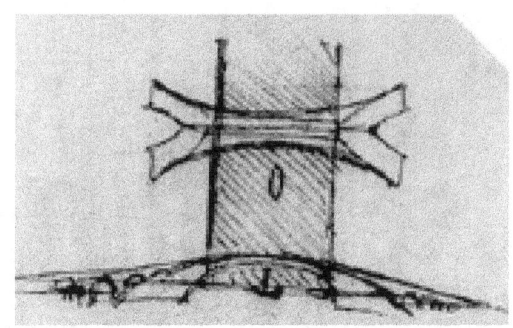

1. I have a sort of extremely light and strong bridges, adapted to be most easily carried, and with them you may pursue, and at any time flee from the enemy; and

others, secure and indestructible by fire and battle, easy and convenient to lift and place. Also methods to burn and destroy those of the enemy.

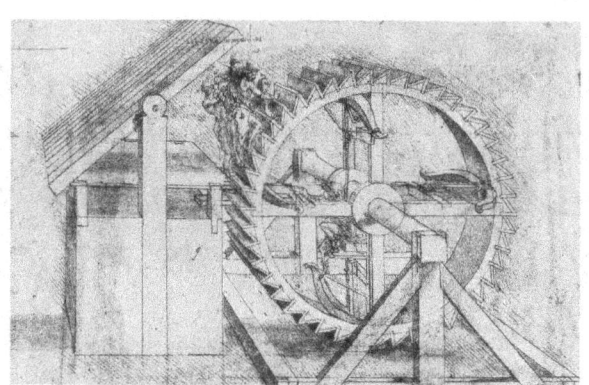

2. I know how, when a place is besieged, to take the water out of the trenches, and make endless variety of bridges, and covered ways and ladders, and other machines pertaining to such expeditions.

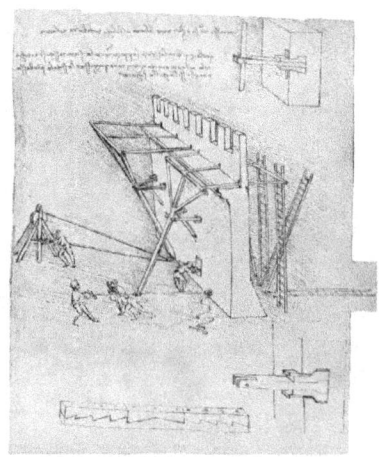

3. Item, If by reason of the height of the banks, or the strength of the place and its position, it is impossible,

when besieging a place, to avail oneself of the plan of bombardment, I have methods for destroying every rock or other fortress, even if it were founded on a rock, etc.

4. Again, I have kinds of mortars; most convenient and easy to carry; and with these can fling small stones almost resembling a storm; and with the smoke of these causing great terror to the enemy, to his great detriment and confusion.

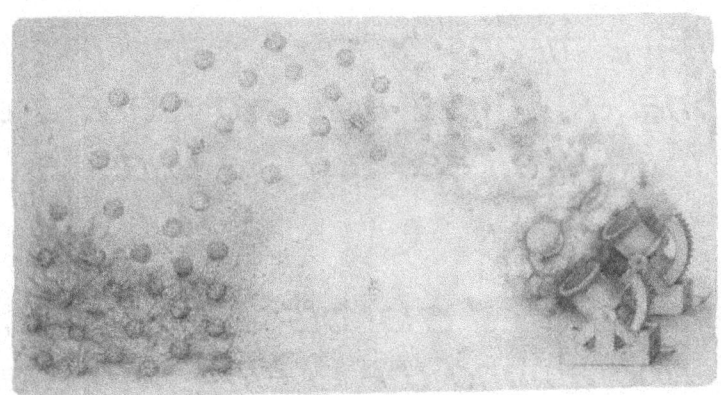

5. And when the fight should be at sea I have kinds of many machines most efficient for offence and defense; and vessels which will resist the attack of the largest guns and powder and fumes.

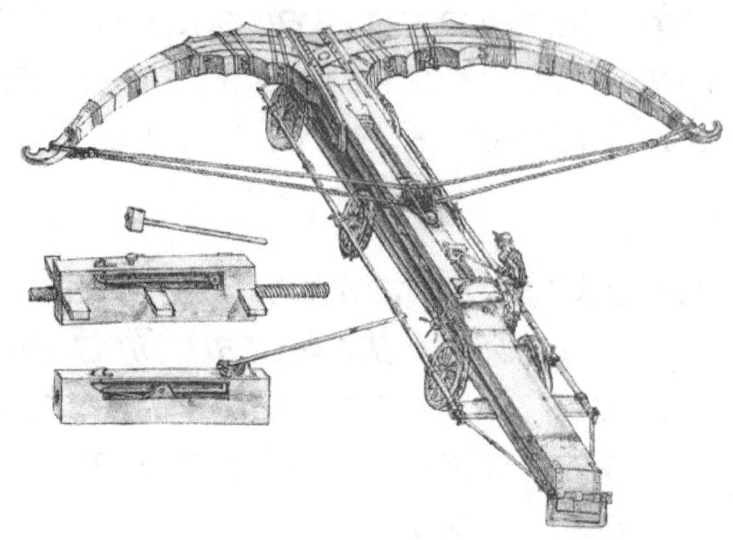

6. Item, I have means by secret and tortuous mines and ways, made without noise to reach a designated spot, even if it were need to pass under a trench or a river.

7. I will make covered chariots, safe and unattackable which, entering among the enemy with their artillery, there is no body of men so great but they would break them. And behind these, infantry could follow quite unhurt and without any hindrance.

8. In case of need I will make big guns, mortars and light ordinance of fine and useful forms, out of the common type.

9. Where the operation of bombardment should fail, I would contrive catapults...and other machines of marvelous efficacy and not in common use. And in short, according to the variety of cases, I can contrive various and endless means of offence and defense...

10. In time of peace I believe I can carry out sculpture in marble, bronze, or clay, and also in painting whatever may be done, and as well as any other, be he whom he may.

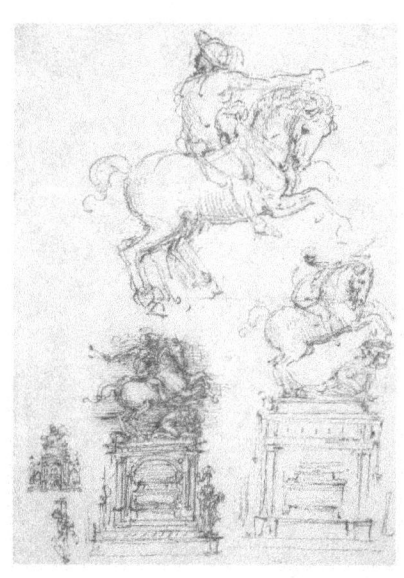

Again the bronze horse may be taken in hand, which is to be to the immortal glory and eternal honour of the prince your father of happy memory, and of the illustrious house of Sforza.

And if any one of the above-named things seem to any one to be impossible or not feasible, I am most ready to make the experiment in your park, or in whatever place may please your Excellency — to whom I commend myself with the utmost humility.

Leonardo da Vinci

← **Byzantine Empire** →				
	← **Holy Roman Empire** →			
		← **Ottoman Empire** →		
← **Middle Ages** →				
		Renaissance		
		Reformation		

Time	500 A.D.	1000	1500	2000+
of Christ			Leonardo	Us

> Byzantine Empire was c.330 to 1453 (from the establishment of Constantinople to its fall).

> Holy Roman Empire – from Charlemagne, c.800, to the end of the Hapsburg line, c.1800.

> Ottoman Empire – from c.1300 – 1922.

> The period of time we call the Middle Ages lasted almost 1000 years, starting with fall of the Roman Empire in the Fifth Century.

> The Renaissance began in the region of Italy c.1350, spreading across Europe from there, and ending c.1550.

> The Protestant Reformation lasted most of the Sixteenth Century.

Map of Italy*

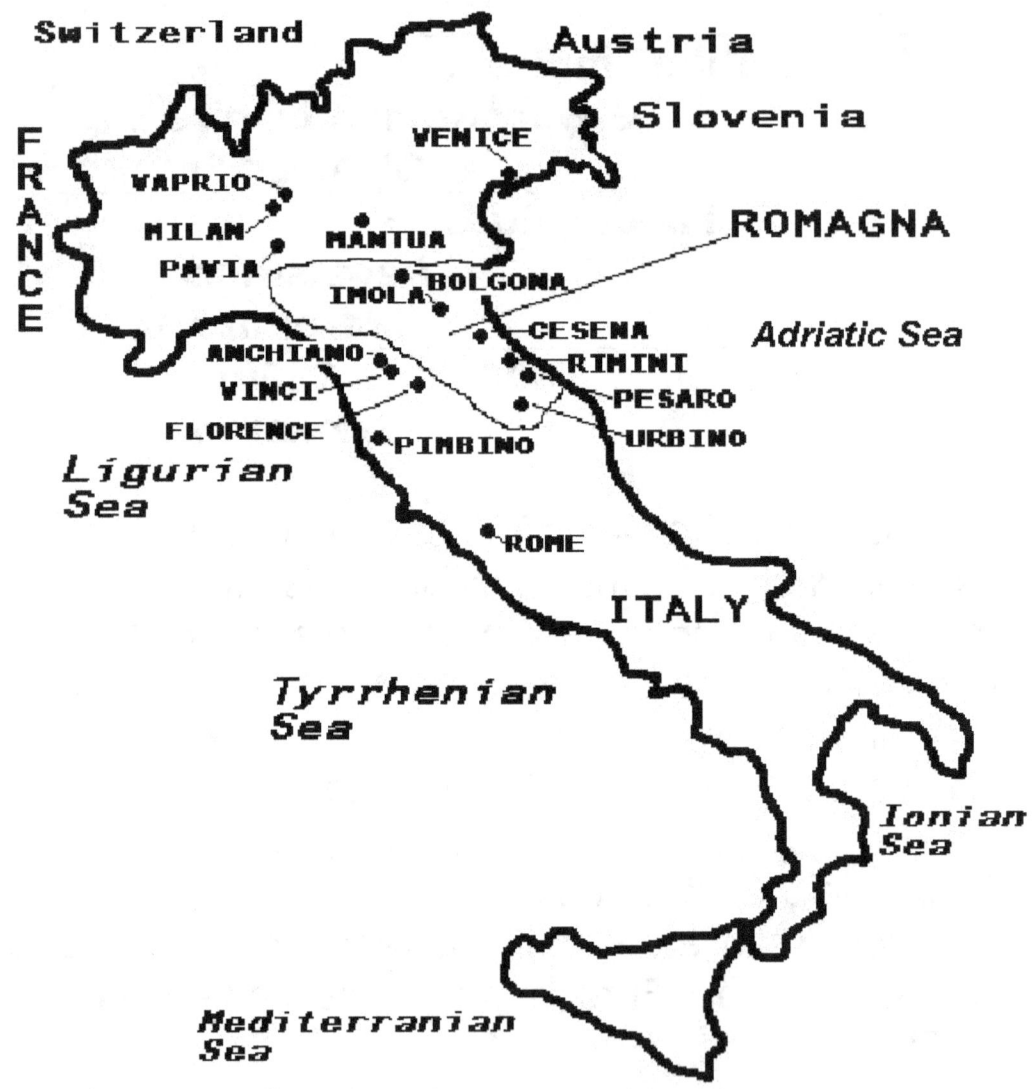

*Shows the places in Italy that Leonardo lived or visited for an extended period of time. (Italy was not a country yet – and many of the cities shown were independent city-states at the time.)

MAP OF EUROPE*

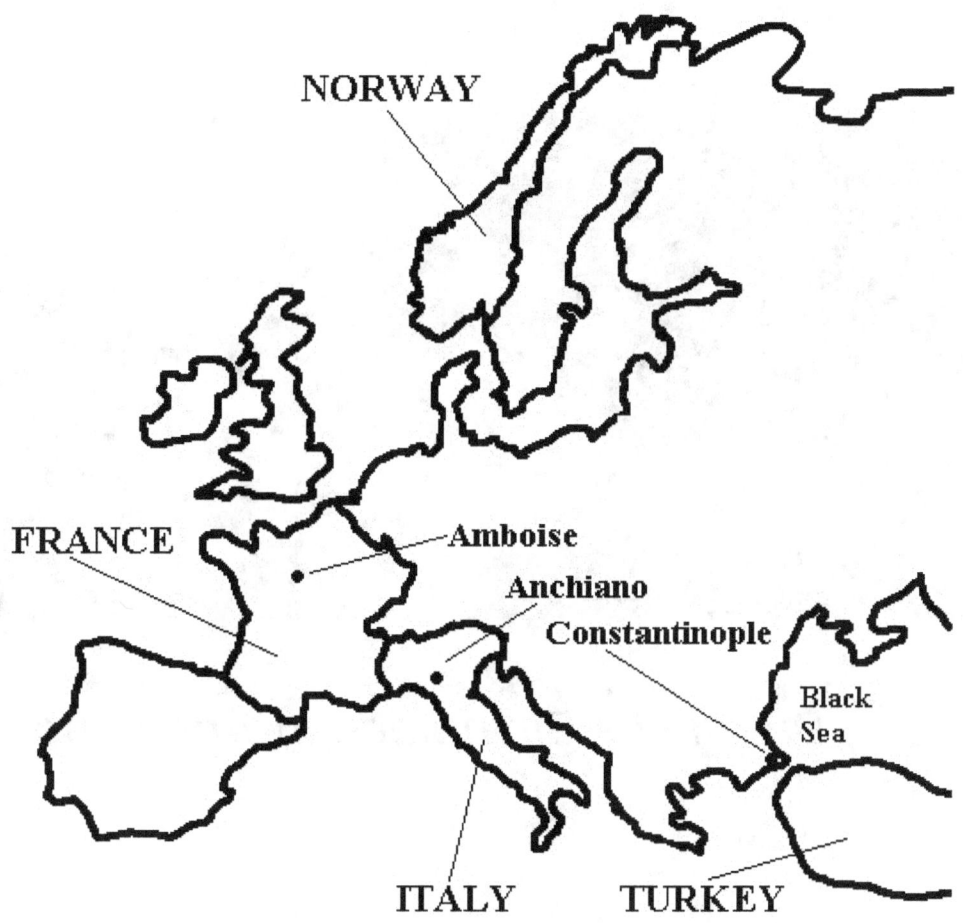

*This map shows the countries in Europe that were an important part of Leonardo's life and legacy, and three important cities: Anchiano, the city of his birth; Amboise, the city of his death; and Constantinople, which is now Istanbul. *(Surprised to see Constantinople and Norway shown here? See the chapter "Leonardo's Bridge" for the answer to that mystery.)*

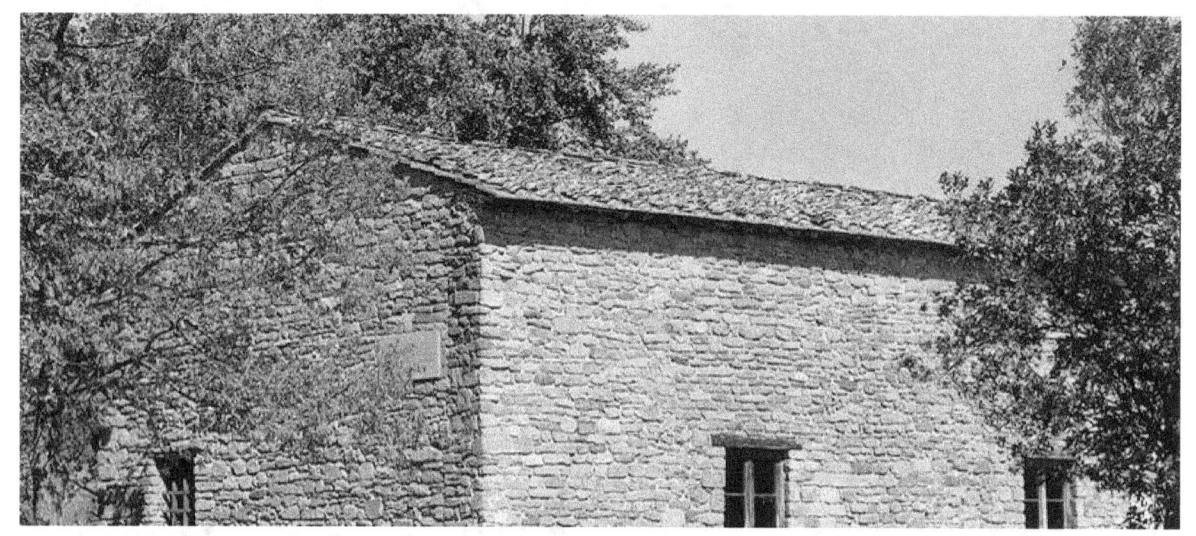

Da Vinci's Birthplace in Anchiano

EARLY YEARS – OVERVIEW:

Leonardo da Vinci was born at the height of the Renaissance in Italy. His early years were not particularly easy for him – he lived first with his mother, and then with his grandparents and uncle, and eventually with his father – changing locations each time. His formal education was very limited until he moved to Florence with his father to apprentice with one of the greatest early artists of the Renaissance, Andrea del Verrocchio.

In addition to this great introduction to art, Leonardo was introduced to Renaissance architecture at this time. Domes were becoming popular in the West, first appearing in Florence, where Leonardo da Vinci spent so much of his early life. In fact, Donato Bramante, one of the greatest dome architects of the day, was working in Florence while Leonardo was there, and Leonardo interacted regularly with him.

In 1472, while still an apprentice, Leonardo was accepted into the local painters' guild. He continued as Verrocchio's apprentice for a while, even after obtaining his status as a "true" painter.

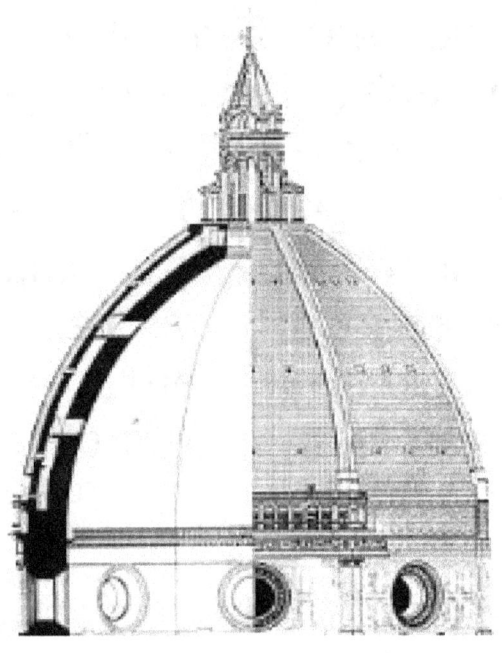

Santa Maria del Fiore in Florence

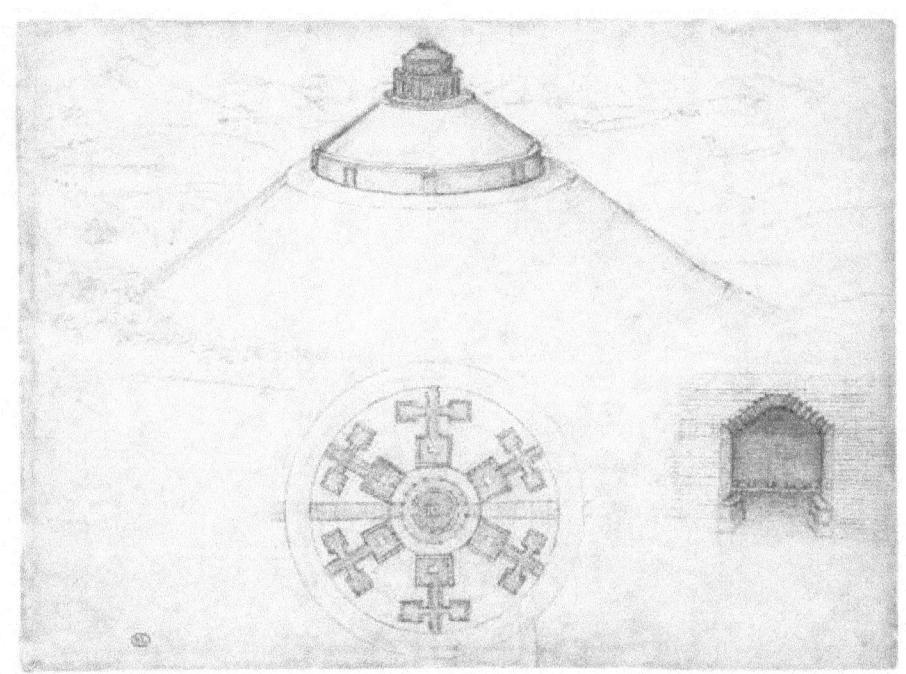

*Leonardo's note to himself:
"First write the treatise on the causes of the giving way of walls and then, separately, treat of the remedies."*

"Simplicity is the ultimate sophistication."

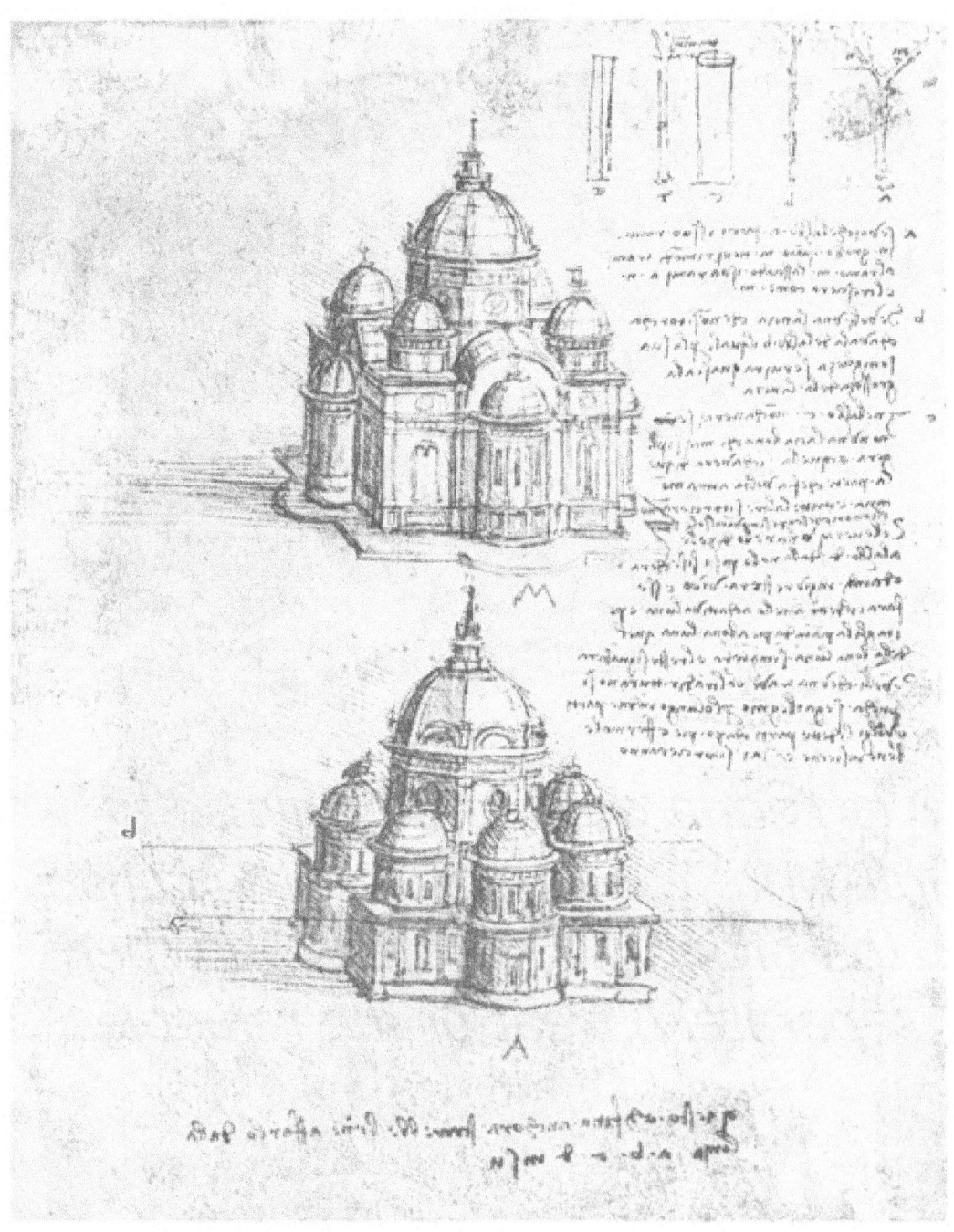

Student Activity:

We discussed architectural styles, some of the problems da Vinci was concerned about (cracks, foundations, etc.), and some of the many things he designed (churches, palaces, canals, locks, cities, and more). The students were directed to use any combination of cardboard, paper, straws, toothpicks, popsicle sticks, paper towel rolls, paper plates and coffee filters to design and make their own building.

Architectural Styles before Da Vinci

1050 – 1250
Romanesque Styles in Architecture

The first European architectural style developed. Romanesque buildings tended to be heavy, with a very gloomy appearance, often with towers at both ends.

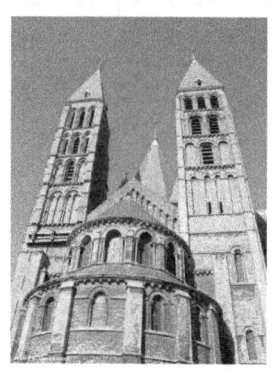

1250 – 1500 Gothic Styles

The Gothic style developed towards the end of the Middle Ages. Gothic buildings were taller, and more graceful. Stained glass windows were popular.

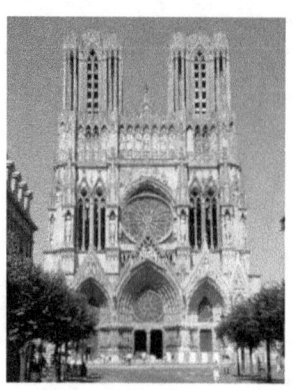

Architecture Approaching
& During Da Vinci's Lifetime

At the beginning of the Fifteenth Century, architecture came to be considered the **supreme** form of art. Symmetry and other geometric balance were important to Renaissance architects, as well as classical proportions. **Domes** became an important part of architecture, starting with Filippo Brunelleschi's work on the dome for the Santa Maria del Fiore in Florence. Brunelleschi developed a new type of dome, in order to make it such a large size. The church was completed in 1432.

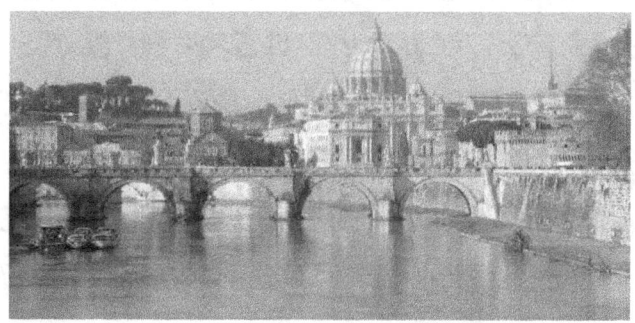

St Peter's Basilica in Rome

In 1447 Pope Nicolas V commissioned work to be done on a new and improved St. Peter's Basilica in Rome. The first architect to work on it was Leon Battista Alberti, but the work was not completed for almost 150 years.

Leonardo, the Architect

From Leonardo's youth, he was fascinated by severe weather – tornados, earthquakes, and the like. He did countless drawings showing the effects of severe storms. Even his architectural studies took weather into consideration – he was intent on planning buildings so that they were strong enough to withstand earthquakes:

> *"That beam which is more than 20 times as long as its greatest thickness will be of brief duration and will break in half...Each beam must pass through its walls and be secured beyond the walls with sufficient chaining, because in consequence of earthquakes the beams are often to seen to come out of the walls and bring down the walls and floors.."*

In the days of da Vinci, architecture was considered a nobler pursuit than painting was, so it is no surprise that da Vinci was also interested in architecture. In his role as an architect, Leonardo's plans were varied – from churches and palaces, to stables, to canals and locks.

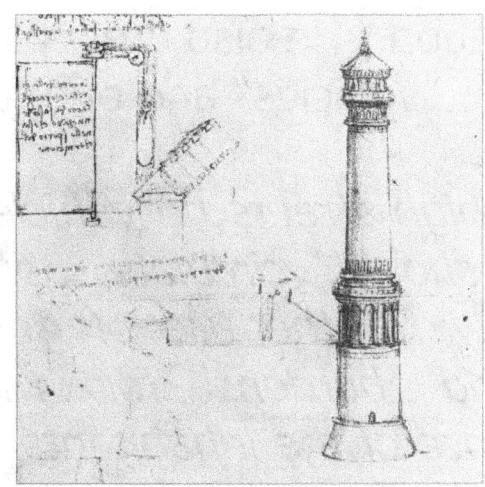

While his plans for most of those remained primarily at the plan level, some of his research and planning in locks and canals was actually carried out in his lifetime.

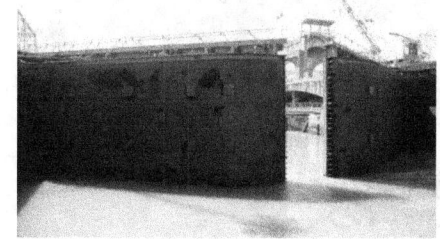

These locks in Panama are similar in design to da Vinci's.

In 1483, Leonardo offered his services to Duke Ludovico of Milan as an engineer, architect, sculptor and painter.

In 1485 and 1486 plagues devastated Milan, killing thousands. In the aftermath, Leonardo collaborated with the Duke to rebuild the city. His plans included ideas for a system of water flowing through the city to improve sanitation.[4] He also drew plans for two sets of streets, one for "vehicles" and one for pedestrians.

> *"By the high streets no vehicles and similar objects should circulate, but they are exclusively for the use of gentlemen. The carts and burdens for the use and convenience of the inhabitants have to go by the low ones."*

> *"Let such a city be built near the sea or a large river in order that the dirt of the city may be carried off by the water."*

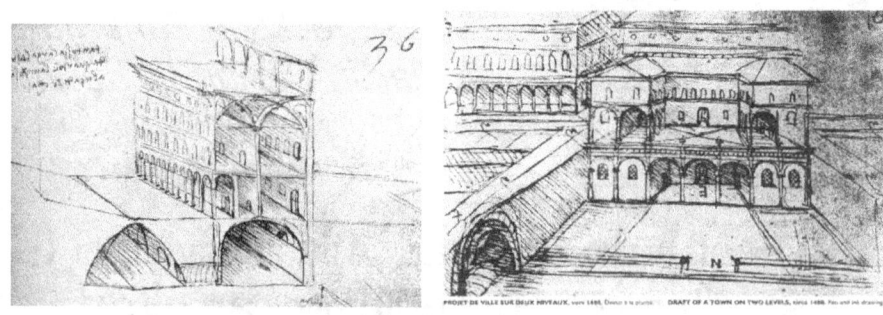

Da Vinci was constantly refining his ideas for how churches should be built. In 1490 Leonardo was sent to Pavia by Duke Ludovico to inspect work on the cathedral there.

---

[4] *Actually a good idea, but never put into effect.*

He also studied cracks in walls, and their causes.

> Note to himself: ""*First write the treatise on the causes of the giving way of walls and then, separately, treat of the remedies...That wall which does not dry uniformly in an equal time, always cracks.*"

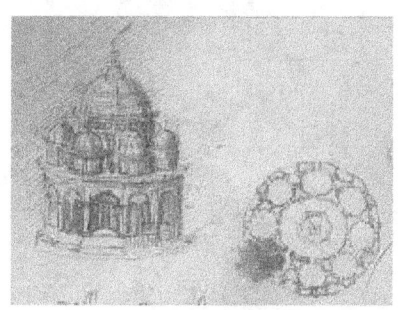

He studied the strength of building materials, domes, foundations, supports, beams, etc. He wrote of "the nature of the arch," and investigated what gave it its strength:

> "*An arch is nothing other than a strength caused by two weaknesses; for the arch in buildings is made up of two segments of a circle, and each of these segments being in itself very weak desires to fall, and as the one withstands the downfall of the other of the two weaknesses are converted into a single strength.*"

Back in Milan, while Leonardo was working on the *Last Supper*, he could observe Donato Bramante, the court's architect, working on the dome of Santa Maria delle Grazie.

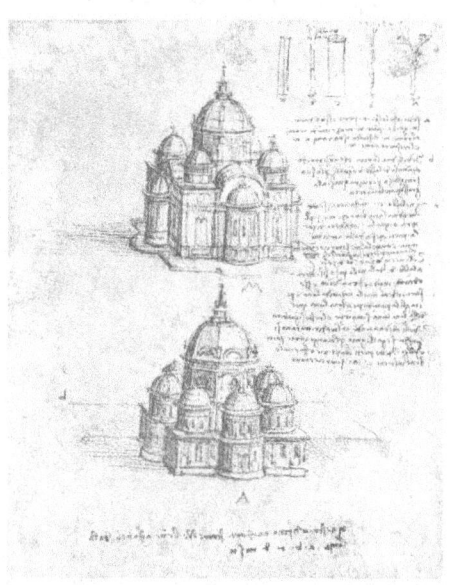

When the dome of another nearby church collapsed, Leonardo's interest in the strength and safety in buildings was piqued.

In 1500, back in Florence, Leonardo was used as an architectural expert in a committee addressing the damages to a church structure, the San Francesco al Monte.

While in Florence, according to his biographer, Giorgio Vasari, Leonardo drew up plans for lifting Church of San Giovanni, and putting a basement under it. He almost, but not quite, convinced the city planners to try his plan.

Another one of Leonardo's architectural suggestions was to put a dance hall only on the bottom floor of a building, so that no one could be crushed beneath it if the weight and stress of the dancing became too much.

He said of foundations:

> *"The first and most important thing is stability. As to the foundations and other public buildings, the depths of the foundations must be at the same proportions to each other as the weight of material which is to be placed upon them."*

In 1503, da Vinci worked on a canal to connect Florence to the sea.

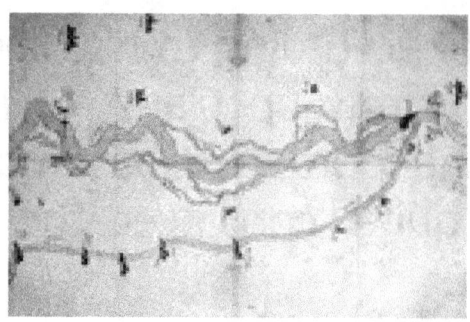

While traveling with Cesare Borgia in 1512, da Vinci served as his military architect and general engineer.

In 1516 da Vinci left Italy for France, to become the "first painter, architect, and mechanic of the King."

So, as you can see, his career as an architect was long and varied.

Leonardo's last few years in Florence were in the employment of Duke Lorenzo de Medici. Then he wrote his extensive letter to Ludovico Sforza, the Duke of Milan, requesting a job with him.

When Leonardo presented himself to the Duke, he took a silver lyre that he had made in the shape of a horse's head as a gift.

Milan was an amazingly busy time in Leonardo's life. In addition to all he did for the Duke, Leonardo started his notebooks, worked on his music, painted *The Last Supper*, and designed an equestrian monument. Leonardo may also have studied in Pavia for a number of months during this period, examining closely both mathematics and science while there.

When Milan fell to French troops in 1499, Duke Ludovico fled. Leonardo da Vinci and his new friend, the mathematician Luca Pacioli, left together, and traveled to Vaprio and to Mantua.

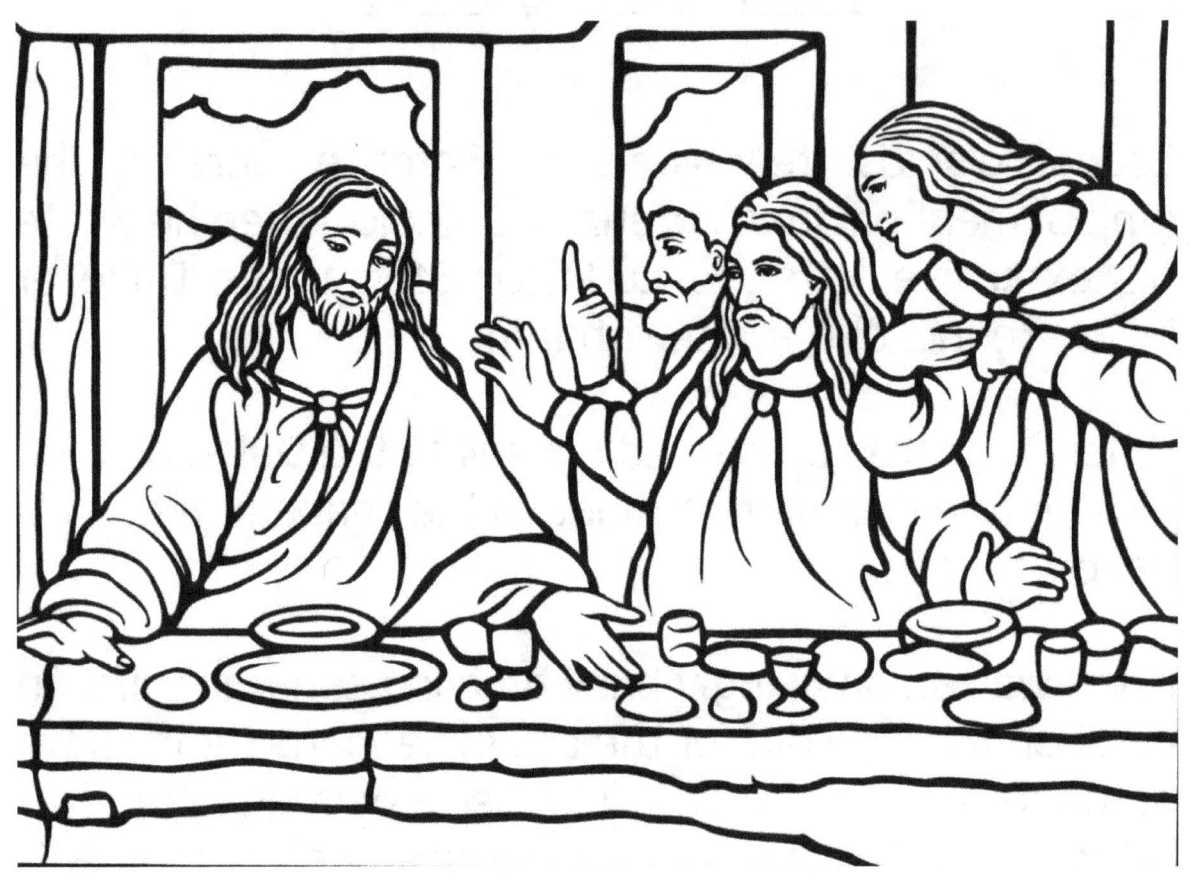

"Art is a major path to knowledge."

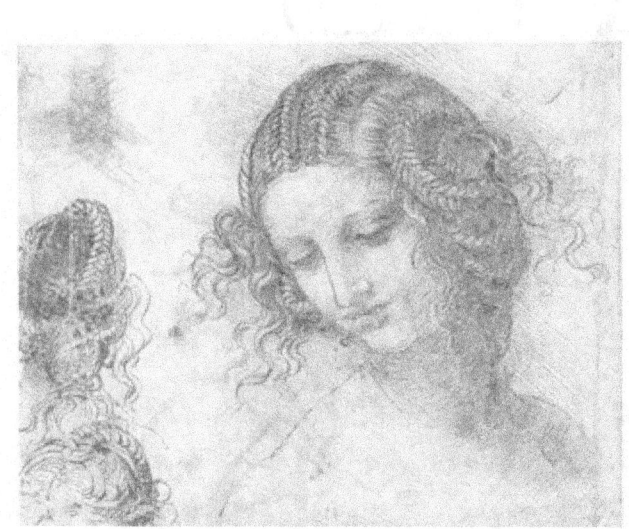

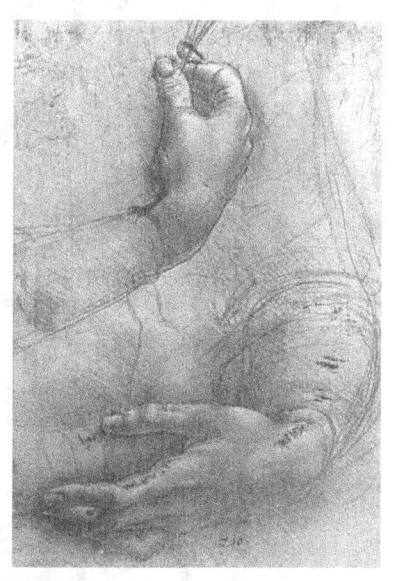

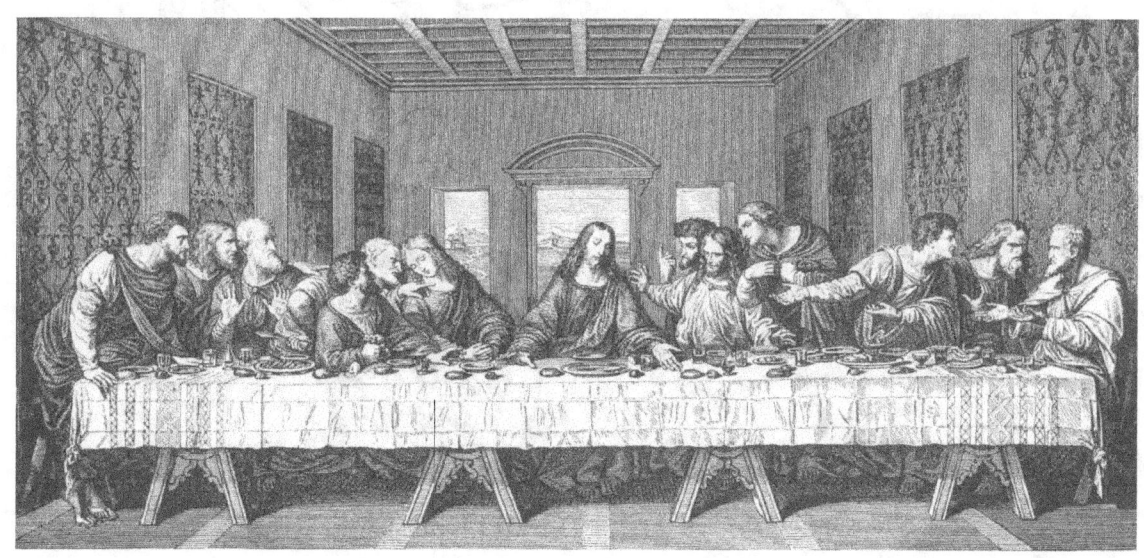

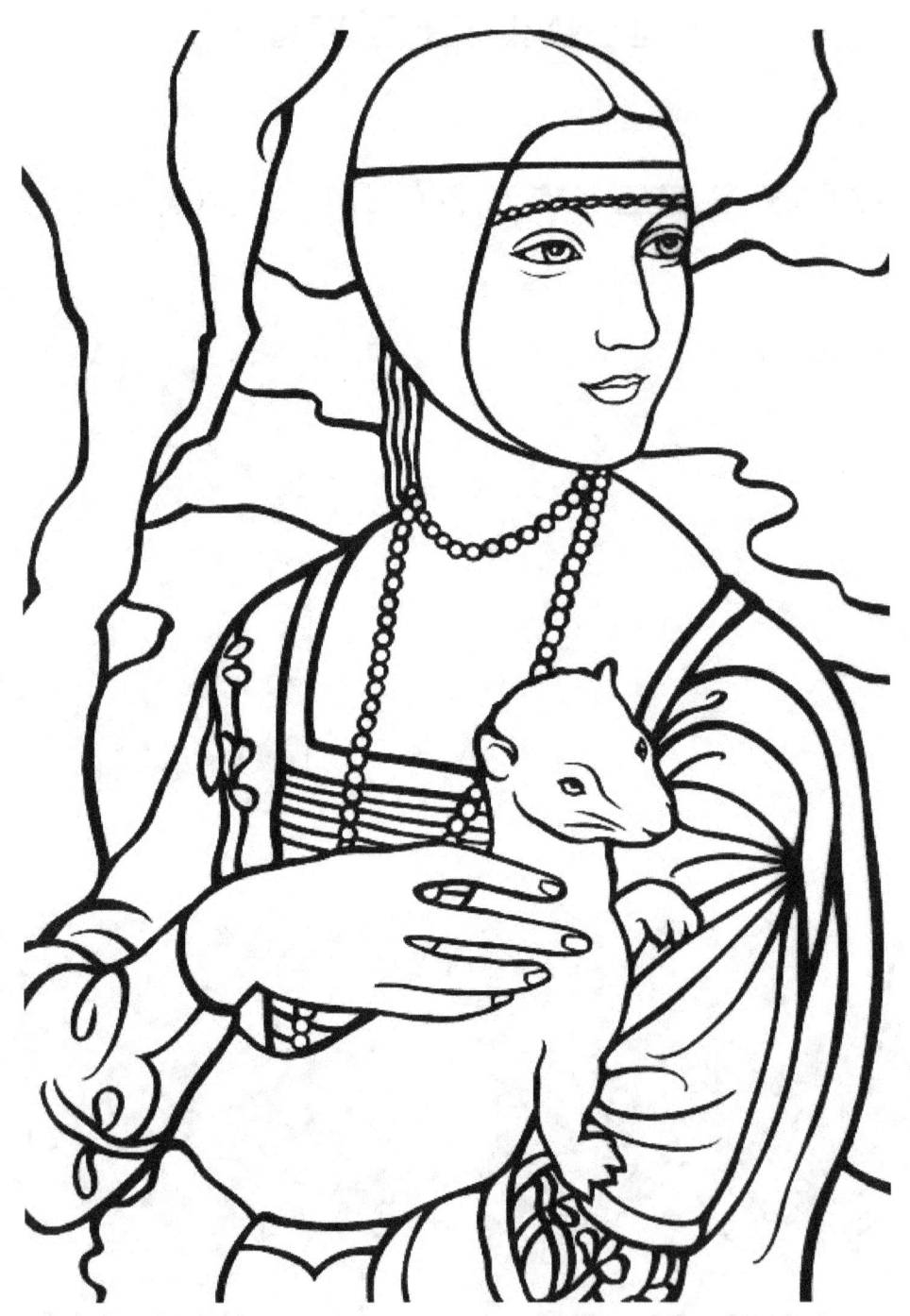

Leonardo's Lady with an Ermine

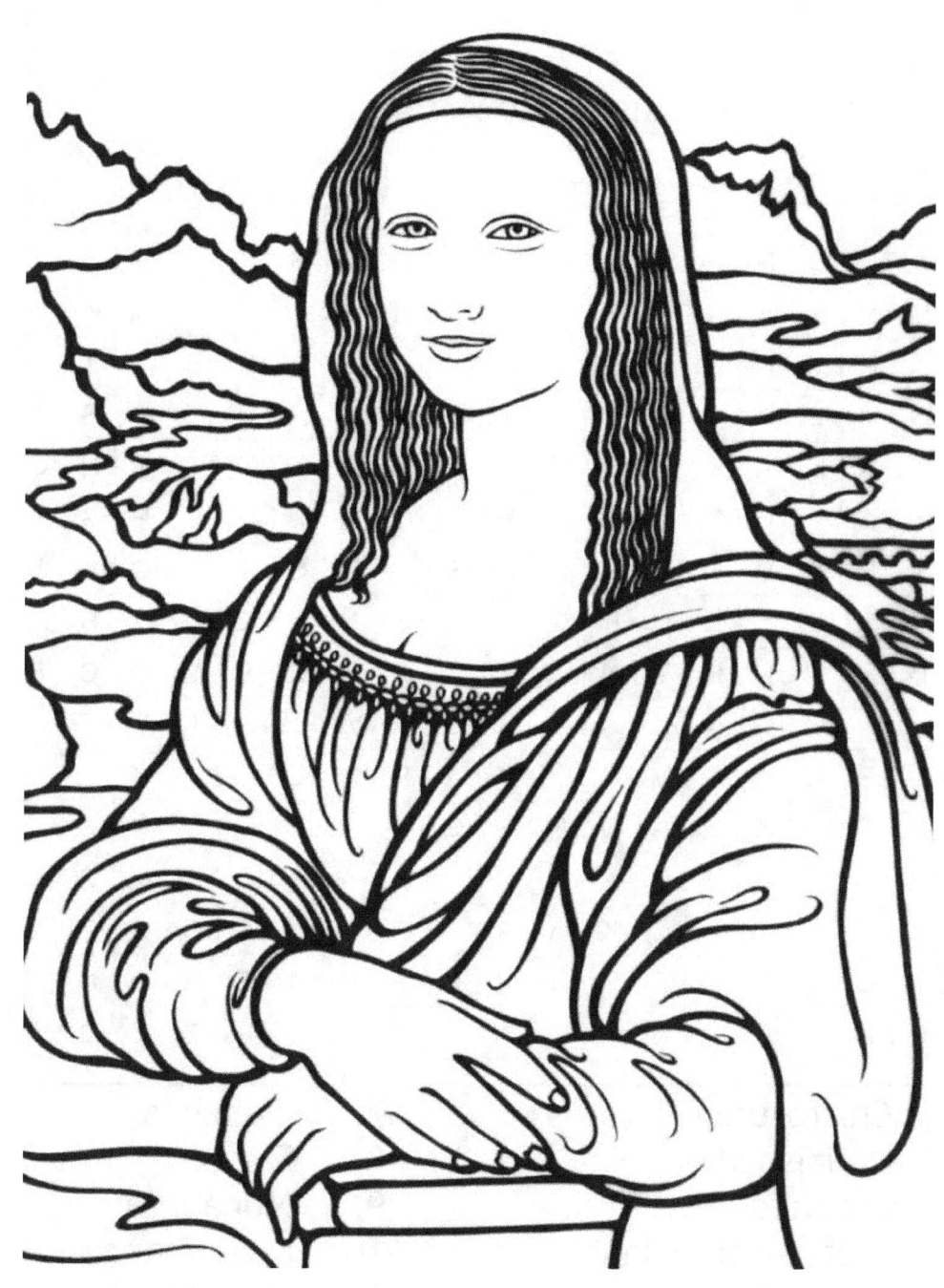

Leonardo's Mona Lisa

Name: _____   Date: _____

Leonardo - Renaissance Artist

F	E	C	N	A	S	S	I	A	N	E	R	J	C	F	J	K	U
F	U	D	P	A	T	G	P	I	D	Q	I	H	K	K	V	Z	G
M	Y	R	F	K	W	C	Q	J	D	H	I	W	Z	P	X	W	C
B	N	M	H	S	Y	D	R	E	C	A	Q	E	U	B	T	K	O
O	V	L	V	V	O	J	H	S	R	I	W	A	R	T	I	S	T
T	R	E	A	T	I	S	E	O	N	P	A	I	N	T	I	N	G
X	C	Y	U	X	I	L	S	P	T	G	M	L	U	S	P	S	J
I	R	J	V	N	L	C	O	W	S	O	M	S	I	F	C	E	L
C	Y	E	I	E	U	R	Q	I	Z	E	N	L	Z	U	G	H	W
D	P	F	N	R	T	N	W	Z	Z	O	R	Q	E	M	G	C	S
J	N	U	O	R	Z	A	A	R	O	K	W	I	R	A	Y	T	Y
U	R	H	A	I	M	C	V	T	A	R	X	L	J	T	K	E	H
B	T	I	K	Q	A	Q	R	S	G	X	C	D	M	O	U	K	Y
Q	T	K	B	B	G	A	A	S	I	L	A	N	O	M	Q	S	N
S	T	N	I	B	C	K	A	P	B	F	R	E	S	C	O	G	G
W	O	I	C	O	R	R	E	V	L	E	D	A	E	R	D	N	A
R	E	P	P	U	S	T	S	A	L	T	W	O	S	Z	Z	S	W

1. Chiarosuro
2. Unfinished
3. Portraits
4. Treatise on Painting
5. Sfumato
6. Cartoons
7. Sketches
8. Fresco
9. Mona Lisa
10. Renaissance
11. Last Supper
12. Artist

36

"These two flutes do not change their tone by leaps as most wind instruments do, but in the manner of the human voice."

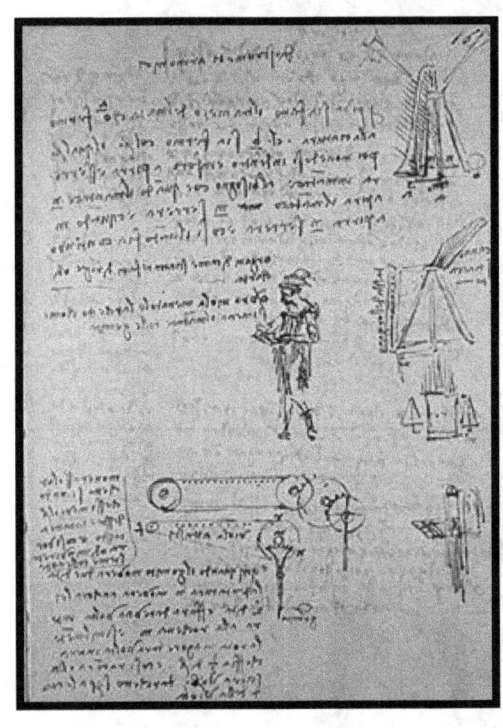

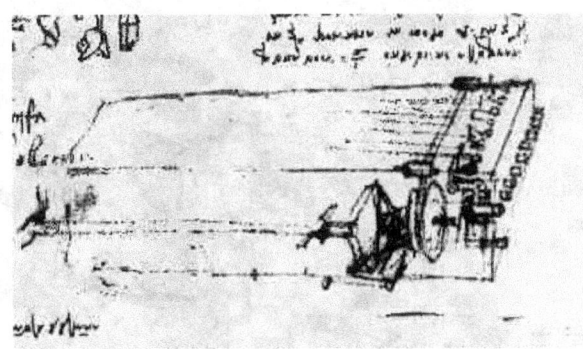

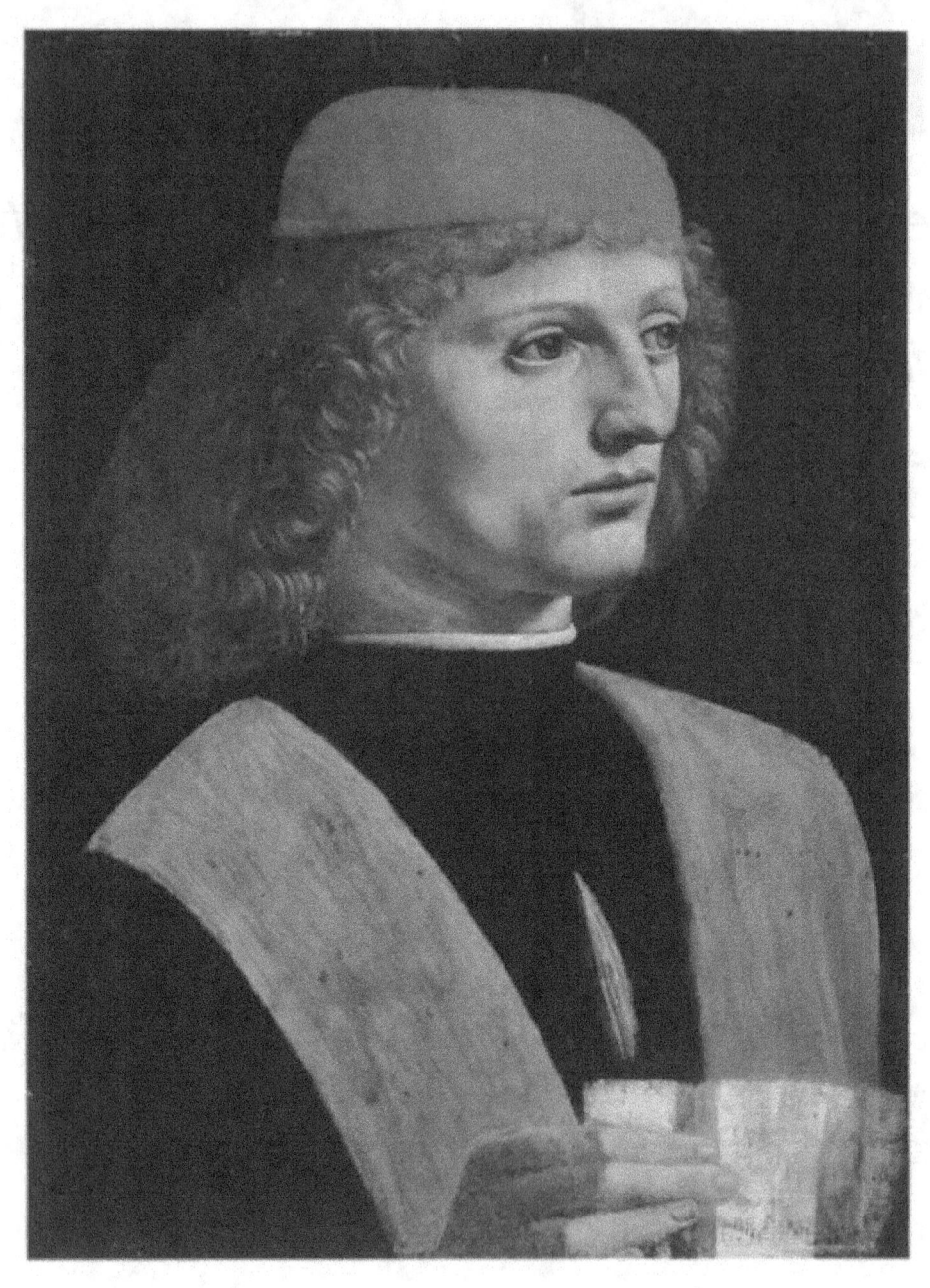

Portrait of a Musician

LEONARDO DA VINCI AND MATHEMATICS

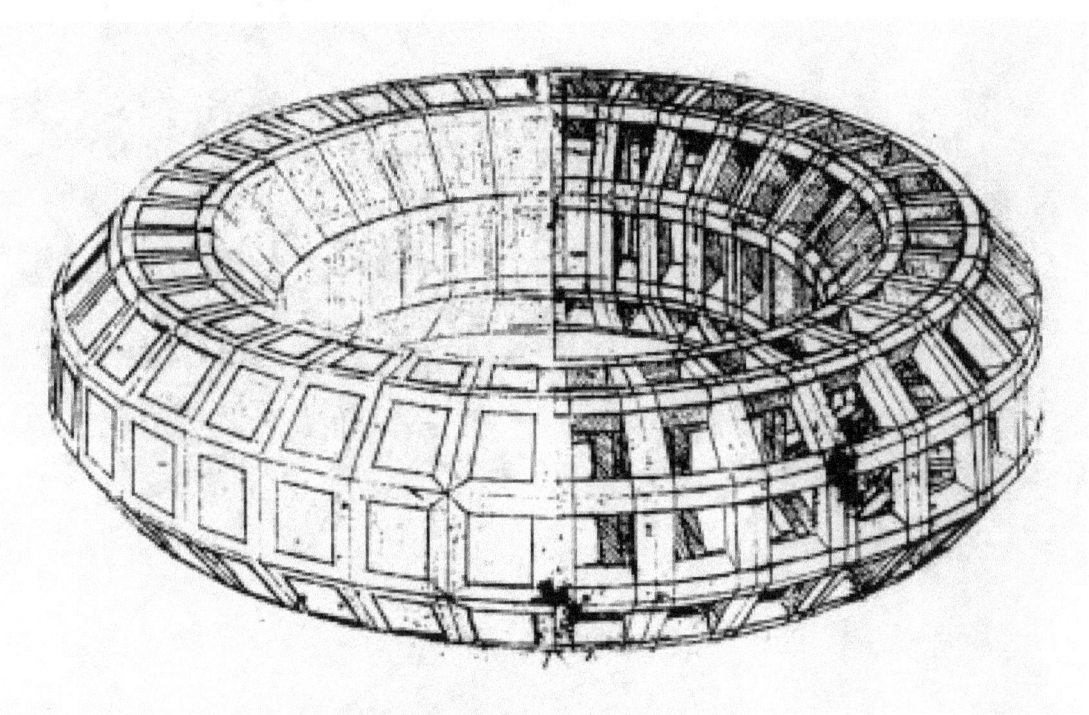

"Let no man who is not a Mathematician read the elements of my work."

"Mechanics are the paradise of mathematical science, because here we come to the fruit of mathematics."

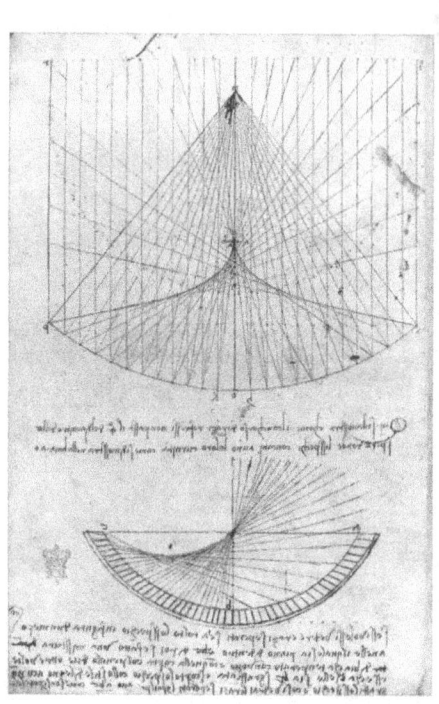

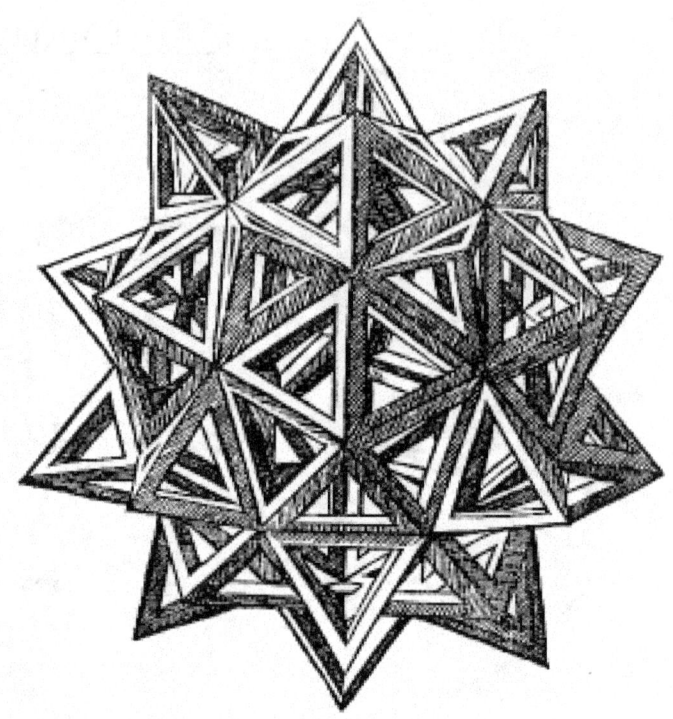

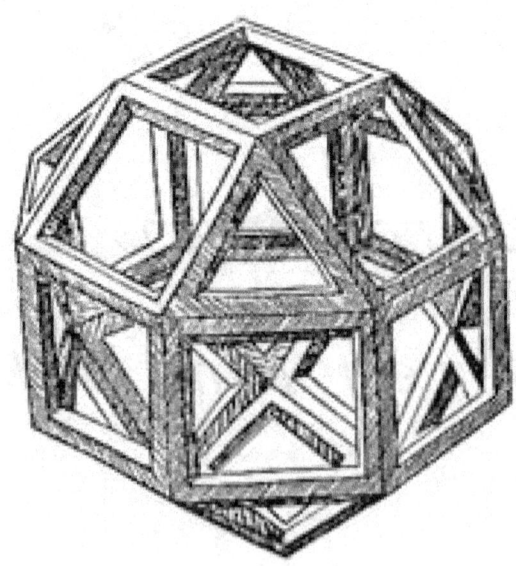

Student Activities:

We started by discussing what made da Vinci so interested in Math...What did he do with it? How did he connect it to Art? Could the students come up with their own art/math connections?

With some of the older students we also talked about Golden Ratios and Fibonacci Numbers.[5]

_____

[5] *Wikipedia has articles on Golden Ratios and Fibonacci Numbers...I would recommend starting with the one of Fibonacci Numbers, it connects the two concepts, and is more readable by "non-mathematicians."*

Euclid first wrote his thirteen book geometry series *Elements* in Greek in about 300 B.C. In 1482, with the new printed press, it became the first printed mathematics book – and was now readily available in Latin. Da Vinci taught himself Latin as an adult, so that he could better read classics such as this. While it would be another 100 years before modern geometry would really come about, in da Vinci's day interest was slowly being rekindled.

Leonardo met Luca Pacioli, a traveling monk about that same time. When Leonardo began designing his famous horse statue, Pacioli helped him with the mathematical problems he faced.

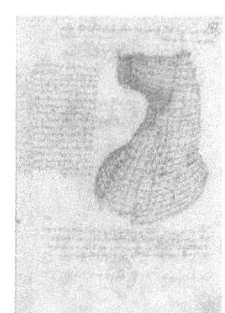

When Pacioli republished his geometry treatise, *De Divina Proportione* ("*On Divine Proportion*") in 1509, it was complete with sixty illustrations by Leonardo da Vinci's (the first of Leonardo's works to ever be published).

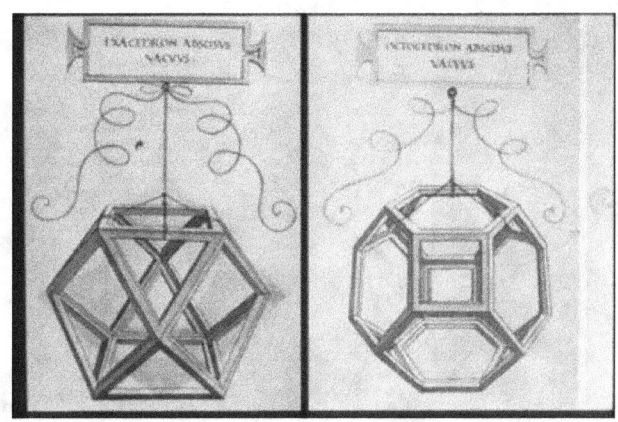

In Leonardo's mind, mathematics went hand in hand with both art and science, and could not really be separated totally from either of them. But for a time, Leonardo was more focused on his mathematics studies than he was on his painting.

> *"The elements of mathematics, that is to say number and measure, termed arithmetic and geometry, discourse with supreme truth on discontinuous and continuous quantities. Here no one argues that twice three makes more or less than six, nor that a triangle has angles smaller than two right angles, but with eternal silence, every dissension is destroyed, and in tranquility these sciences are relished by their devotees."*

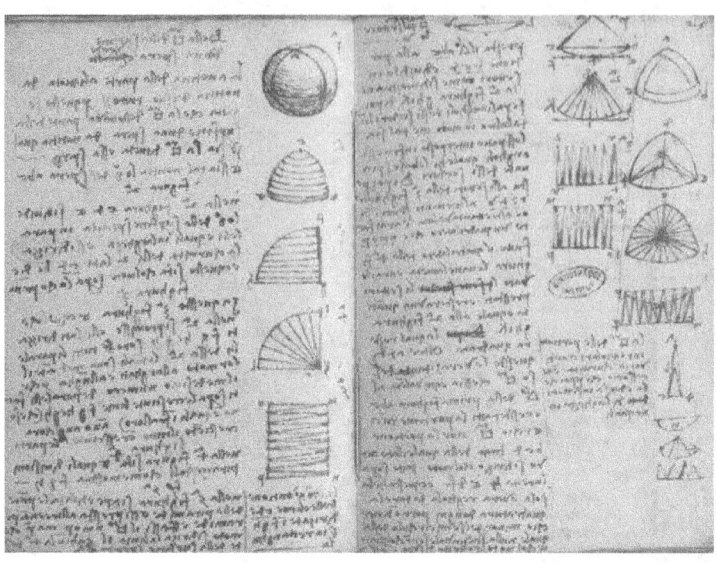

"The other proof which Plato gave to those of Delos is not geometry, because you proceed by the instrument of compasses and ruler, and experience shows it to us. But this is an occupation of the mind and as a consequence, geometry."

The night of St. Andrew's day, I came to the end of the squaring of the circle and it was the end of the night and of the paper on which I was writing. It was concluded at the end of the hour.

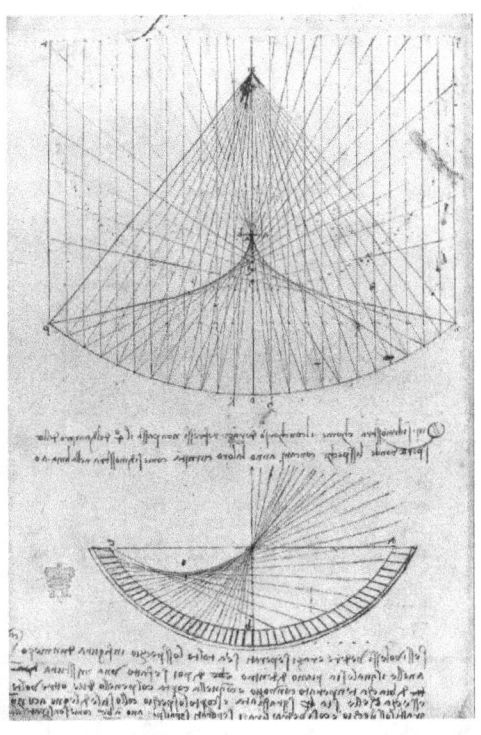

So we should not be surprised to learn that one of Leonardo's patrons complained: "He is so much distracted from painting by his mathematical experiments as to become intolerant of the brush."

"Mechanics is the paradise of the mathematical sciences because by means of it one comes to the fruits of mathematics."

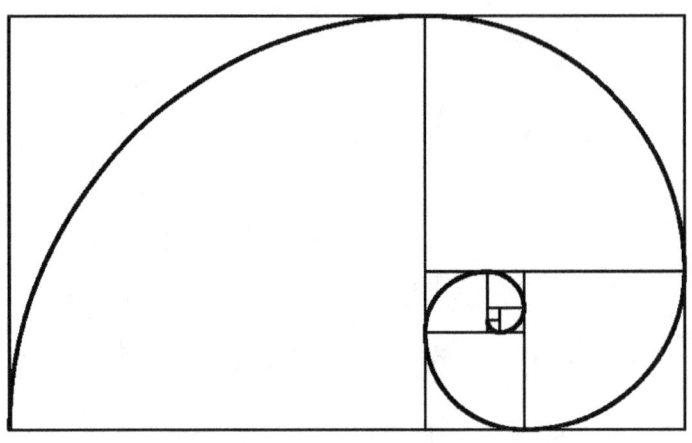

A Fibonacci Spiral

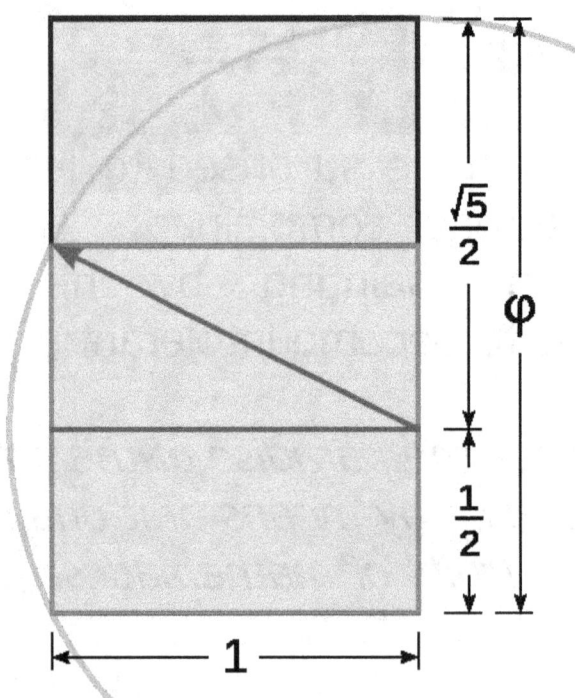

Golden Ratios are used to make Golden Rectangles.

46

"From science is born creative action, which is of much more value."

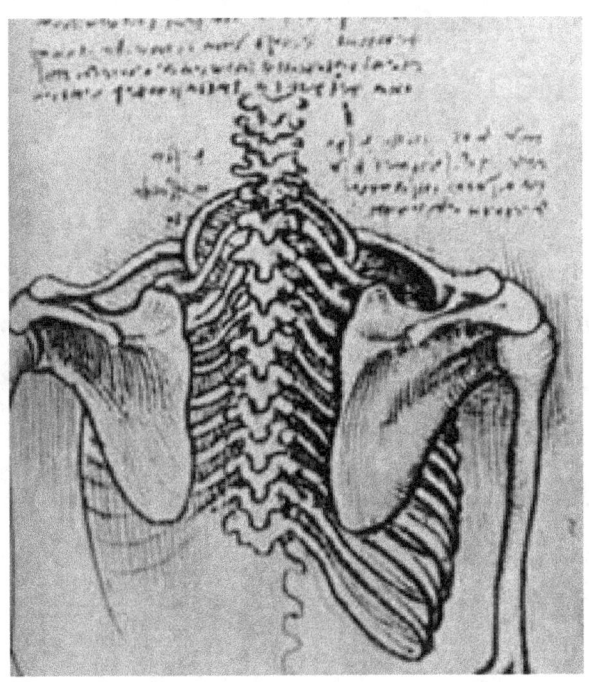

Leonardo da Vinci is considered by many to be the first modern scientist.

He:
- Observed
- Questioned
- Made hypotheses
- Experimented

Leonardo
- Measured:

  Humidity

  Altitude

  Distance traveled

  Speed of wind

  Motion of water

  Intensity of Light

He studied:
- Anatomy

  He wrote of the human body: *"A wonderful instrument, the invention of the supreme master."*

- Astronomy

  "I say that as the moon has no light in itself and yet is luminous, it is inevitable but that its light is caused by some other body."

- Botany

  "A leaf always turns its upper side towards the sky so that it may better receive, on all its surface, the dew which drops gently from the atmosphere."

- Creation vs. Evolution

  "Why do we find the bones of great fishes and oysters and corals and various other shells and sea-snails on the high summits of mountains by the sea, just as we find them in low seas?"

- Geology

  "Mountains are made by the currents of rivers. Mountains are destroyed by the currents of rivers.

- Mechanics

    "Mechanics are the paradise of mathematical science, because here we come to the fruit of mathematics."

- Optics

    "When both eyes direct the pyramid of sight to an object, that object becomes clearly seen and comprehended by the eyes."

- Zoology

    "The smallest feline is a masterpiece."

- and much more...

LEONARDO'S NOTEBOOKS

"He labored much more by his word than in fact or deed."[6]—Giorgio Vasari

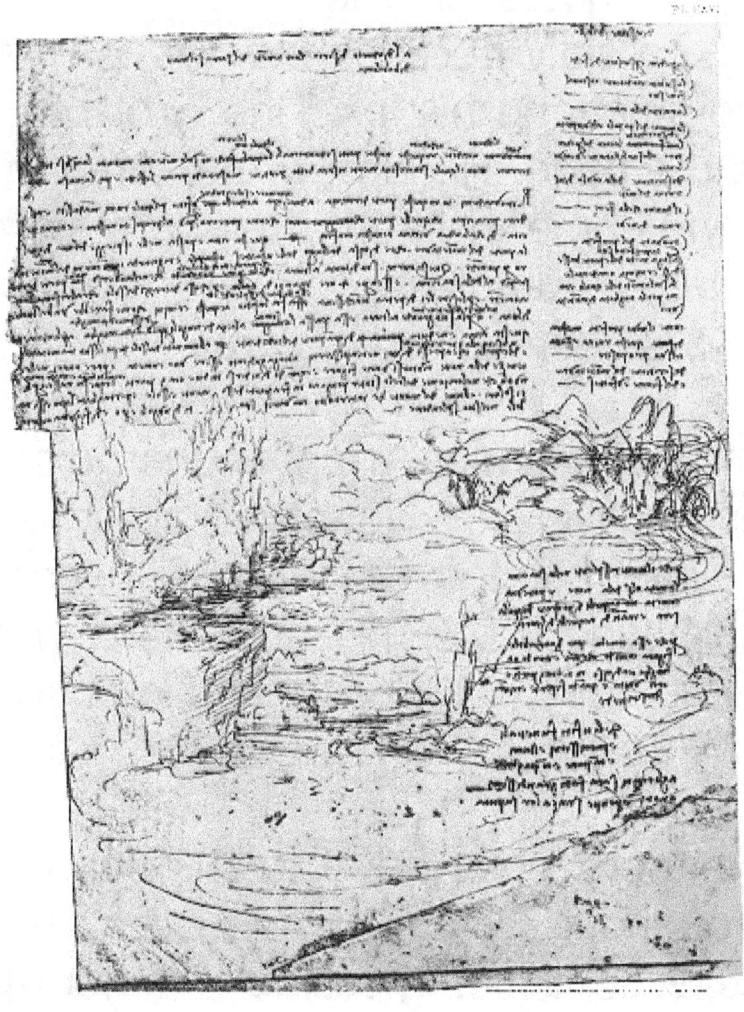

---

[6] *In the early biography of Leonardo da Vinci by Giorgio Vasari.*

Leonardo made a practice of always carrying a small notebook with him and then copying his notes, sketches, etc. onto larger sheets each evening.

Leonardo's notebooks were unique for many reasons: He started his notes on the "back page." He wrote backwards, possibly because he was left-handed and could avoid smearing his ink if he wrote from right to left across the page. He also wrote some of his notes in Italian and some in Latin after he started learning that language. Needless to say, deciphering his notebooks has been an arduous task!

More than 7,000 pages from Leonardo's notebooks have been recovered.[7] No other artist or scientist, before or since, has left the kind of "paper trail" that Leonardo da Vinci left – his notebooks were like his journal, sketchbook, scrapbook, and log book, all rolled into one.

Pages from notebooks have been found in obscure places throughout Europe, some even recently, and now the collections mostly reside in major museums in

---

[7] *It is believed that there were at least 14,000 pages originally.*

Leonardo's notebooks were generally unorganized, usually consisting of loose pages, that he only occasionally bound himself. They contained notes about four major categories: anatomy, architecture, mechanics, and painting. His notebooks also included:

- o astronomy
- o botany
- o drafts of letters
- o geology
- o geography
- o invention plans
- o lists of books
- o maps he had drawn
- o menus from what he had eaten recently
- o notes from borrowed books
- o quotes
- o shopping lists
- o sketches for paintings he was working on
- o water
- o weapons
- o work with weights

Leonardo's Notebooks

R	S	A	E	A	A	F	Y	H	L	N	R	H	S	M	Y	N	H	A
U	Q	I	F	N	T	G	A	C	H	Q	A	F	R	P	H	J	P	U
S	Z	N	N	Y	O	X	B	A	G	V	B	U	Y	J	N	I	S	I
T	A	N	K	L	Y	O	I	C	E	E	G	T	W	A	T	E	R	N
H	Z	J	O	M	T	F	W	Q	O	R	E	N	Y	K	H	G	E	V
G	L	E	Y	A	P	E	Z	U	G	P	W	T	E	S	W	R	T	E
I	G	K	N	Z	A	L	D	Z	R	A	O	P	K	D	X	M	T	N
E	B	Y	S	P	O	U	O	U	A	Q	Z	B	H	K	B	V	E	T
W	J	S	O	E	Y	O	X	S	P	P	I	M	M	F	A	V	L	I
H	M	N	K	J	H	M	K	J	H	S	B	J	R	J	Y	G	F	O
T	S	N	L	O	T	C	O	Y	Y	A	P	D	C	X	J	S	O	N
I	N	W	O	Y	O	I	T	N	P	A	V	A	X	N	U	R	S	P
W	T	T	E	T	E	B	H	E	O	Q	N	H	M	N	M	O	T	L
K	P	X	L	N	E	L	E	O	K	R	A	I	E	P	Q	R	F	A
O	X	L	O	T	M	S	I	T	F	S	T	M	Z	J	K	Z	A	N
W	L	I	S	T	S	O	F	B	O	O	K	S	Z	U	C	L	R	S
L	A	N	V	H	V	P	N	X	B	N	T	T	A	F	N	Q	D	R

1. Menus
2. Sketches
3. Geography
4. Botany
5. Drafts of Letters
6. Geology

7. Lists of Books
8. Maps
9. Weapons
10. Astronomy
11. Invention Plans
12. Notes

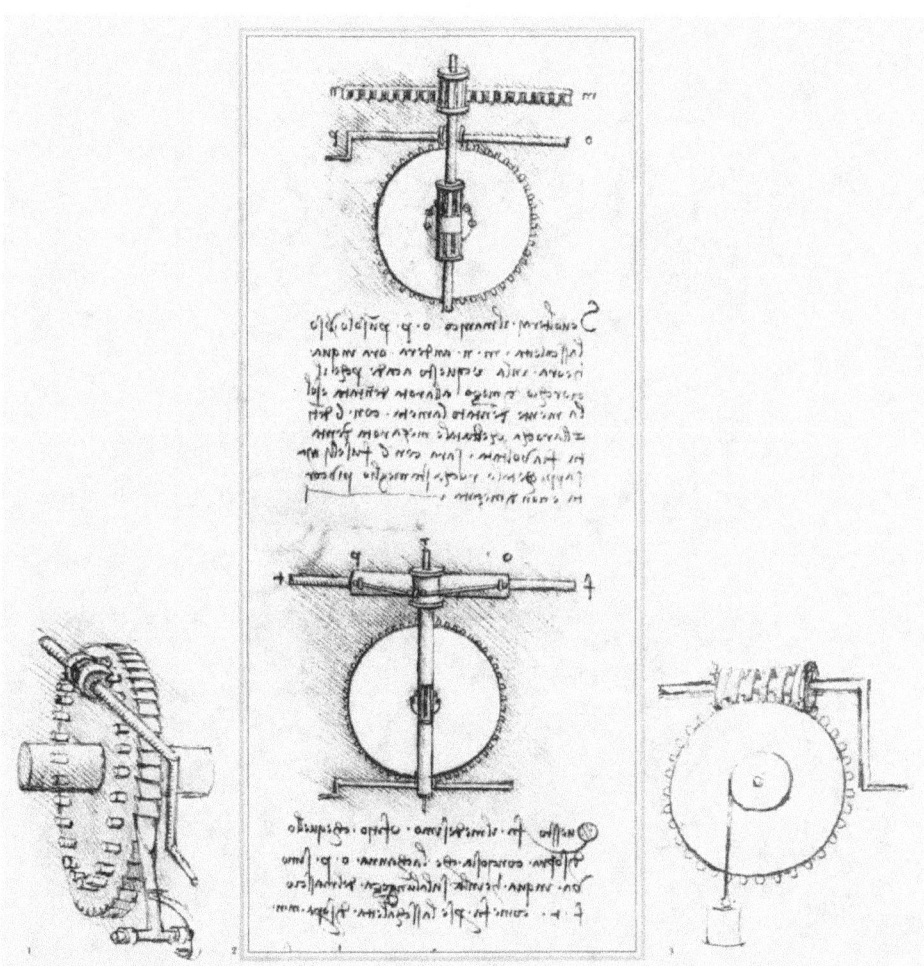

The perseverance to pursue it and to invent such things...is found in few people."

"I have been impressed with the urgency of doing. Knowing is not enough; we must apply. Being willing is not enough; we must do."

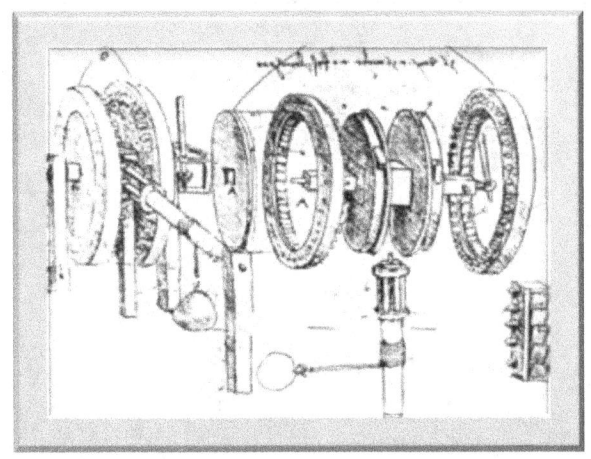

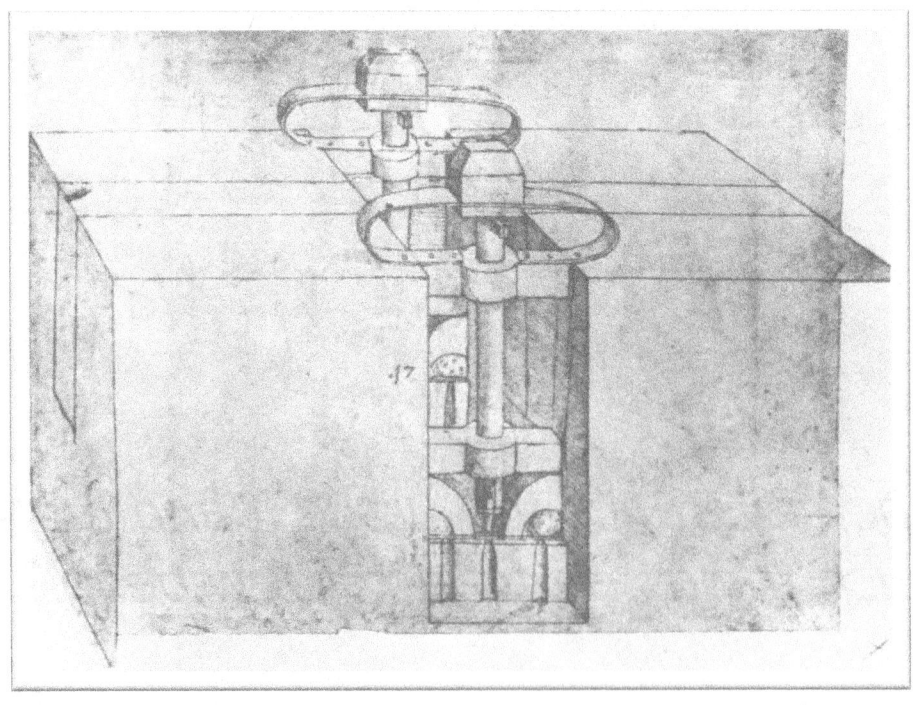

Leonardo's "Inventions"

J	P	Q	S	I	T	N	E	Y	E	G	L	A	S	S	E	S
L	K	A	U	T	X	S	Y	I	L	F	T	H	H	M	M	Z
W	Y	O	D	O	X	U	H	E	V	U	D	R	Q	E	T	S
K	W	O	H	D	I	M	E	J	G	P	H	F	C	Y	E	G
A	E	V	I	P	L	H	J	F	L	R	U	H	A	S	W	I
I	R	O	A	H	W	E	B	M	A	I	A	Z	N	Y	C	A
Y	C	W	F	R	U	M	B	S	U	N	Y	E	L	E	O	N
D	S	N	E	D	M	Q	R	O	I	B	L	U	T	P	B	T
H	L	T	S	S	O	L	V	C	A	T	Z	J	L	O	I	C
N	A	W	U	Y	A	Q	A	V	C	T	F	L	V	C	C	R
W	I	W	H	E	E	L	B	A	R	R	O	W	H	S	Y	O
Z	R	U	D	S	D	E	T	J	J	B	Z	K	W	E	C	S
C	E	P	T	R	U	N	U	K	A	B	Y	F	Y	L	L	S
I	A	G	U	G	O	Z	D	N	P	Y	Q	Z	S	E	E	B
K	D	M	C	C	N	R	J	N	K	S	K	G	R	T	Q	O
O	D	S	P	I	N	N	I	N	G	W	H	E	E	L	E	W

1. Bicycle
2. Paddleboat
3. Water Wheel
4. Contact Lenses
5. Giant Crossbow
6. Mechanical Drum
7. Wheelbarrow
8. Spinning Wheel
9. Eye Glasses
10. Aerial Screw
11. Telescope

Student Activity:

The assignment was to figure out a problem that needed to be solved and design a machine using at least one of the following: wheels, pulleys, gears, screws, or levers.

After sketching creative and interesting ideas, we worked on our own designs/models of the different inventions using various amounts of cardboard, cardboard rolls, craft sticks, straws, paper clips, coffee filters, foil sheets, old CDs, computer paper, yarn, rubber bands, and tape.

Leonardo da Vinci was a great artist – but he was also a great scientist and inventor. In fact, he could be rightly called the first modern-day scientist. He was always investigating the world around him – and looking for ways to make things work better. He studied the machines already being used, and constantly sought to understand them. He was one of the first to study friction and its effect on machines.

As most are now, his machines were comprised of various combinations of:
> ⇒wheels and axles
> ⇒pulleys
> ⇒wedges
> ⇒screws
> ⇒levers
> ⇒gears
> ⇒springs

He used many of these in new and unusual ways, and often in plans that went beyond the materials available in his day. Leonardo was always looking for new ways to combine these into new machines. He wanted to save people time with many of his inventions. He designed and sometimes even made flying machines, war machines, water machines, and work machines.

Many of Leonardo's "inventions" never went beyond the planning stage during his lifetime, often because he was "ahead of his time." Centuries later, though, many of his ideas were actually built: the helicopter, the tank, the machine gun, the parachute, the wheelbarrow – all existed in Leonardo's mind and notebooks long before they came to be.

In fact, one hundred years before Galileo used a telescope to look at the stars, Leonardo was considering the possibility of "making glasses with which...to view the moon at an enlarged size." And because of his skills as an artist, his detailed sketches often showed his ideas very clearly.

His plans were varied, including a wide variety of ideas for a(n)

- Alarm Clock
- Aerial Screw
- Automatic Roasting Spit
- Double Crane
- Drilling Machine
- Eye Glasses
- Lens Grinding Machine (for mirrors)
- Locks for Canals
- Mechanical Drum
- Monkey Wrench
- Oil Lamp that gave out brighter light
- Paddle Boat
- Parachute
- Projector
- Pulleys
- Revolving Crane
- Screw-thread Cutter
- Self-propelled Car
- Spinning Wheel improvements
- Telescope
- Water Pump
- Water Wheel
- Wheel Barrow

   to name "a few"...

A Specific Invention – A Mint Machine:

Leonardo da Vinci moved to Rome under the patronage of Giuliano de Medici, brother of Pope Leo X. While there, Leonardo designed a machine for the Pope to mint coins. Banking and coin minting had almost disappeared completely in Europe during the Middle Ages; at the time of the Renaissance, both were slowly coming back.

Surprisingly, the invention of the printing press led first to advancements in minting coins, rather than printing bills. Leonardo used the same principles from the printing press (which had borrowed ideas from grape presses) to develop his machine to mill coins – a method that led to greater uniformity in size and weight.[8]

Of his mint at Rome, Leonardo said, *"It can also be made without a spring. But the screw above must always be joined to the part of the movable sheath...all the coins should be a perfect circle."*

---

[8] *Milled coins also made it more difficult to "shave" the edges of coins.*

A Specific Idea — a "Robot":

One of the things Leonardo tried to invent was a "robot." Of course, Leonardo didn't call his mechanical man a "robot" — that word wouldn't come into usage until 1921, when humanoid robots would appear in a science fiction play, and decades more would pass before one would actually be built.

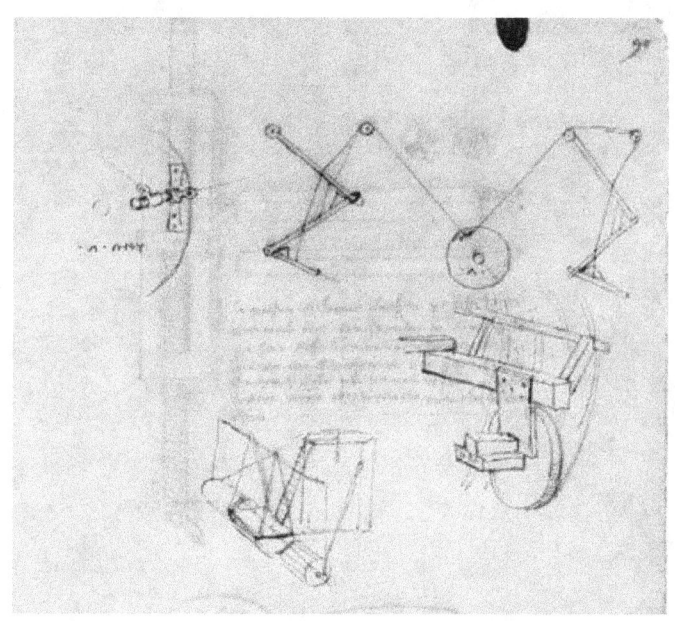

The plans for a humanoid robot in Leonardo's notebooks are dated as early as 1495, making it very probably the first humanoid robot ever designed. There's no proof that Leonardo ever built the robot, though some people argue that he did — but one was built recently, based on his plans.

Other Ideas:

What do you think of when you see the following machines that Leonardo designed? Do you think they would work? Do you think we've done anything similar since he drew these? Can you find how Leonardo used pulleys, screws, wheels, and gears in these designs?

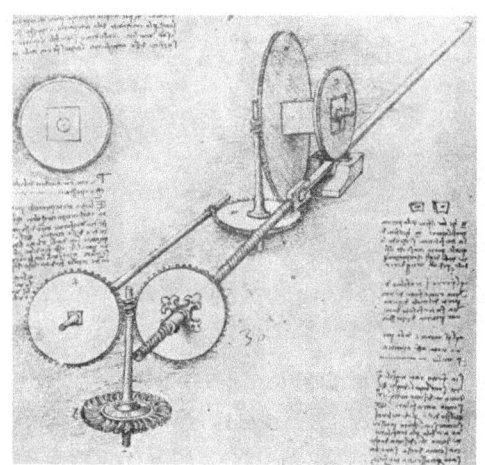 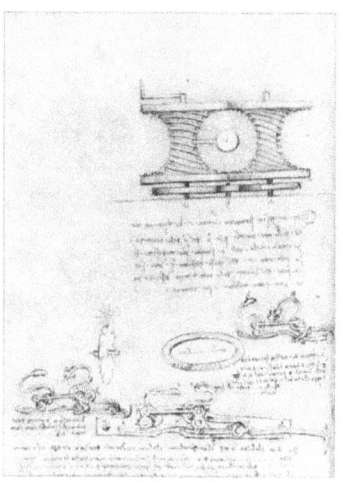

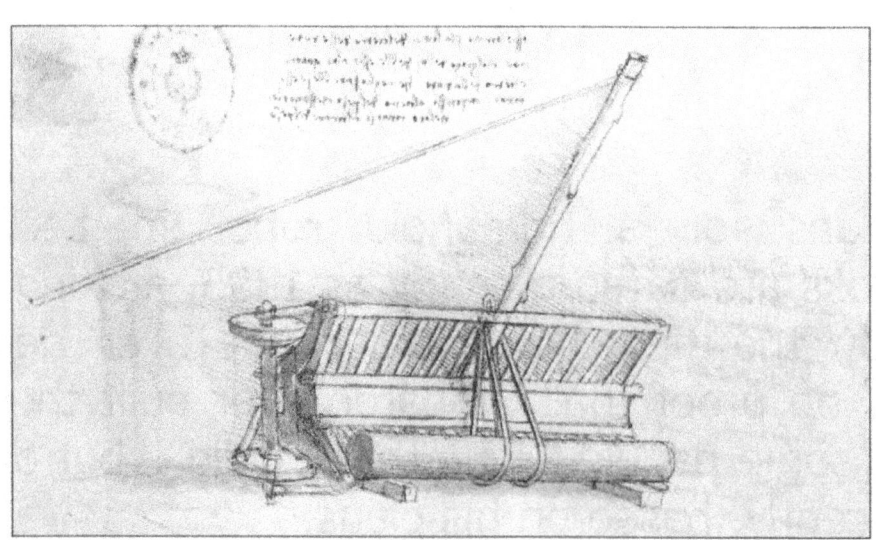

LEONARDO DA VINCI'S HORSE

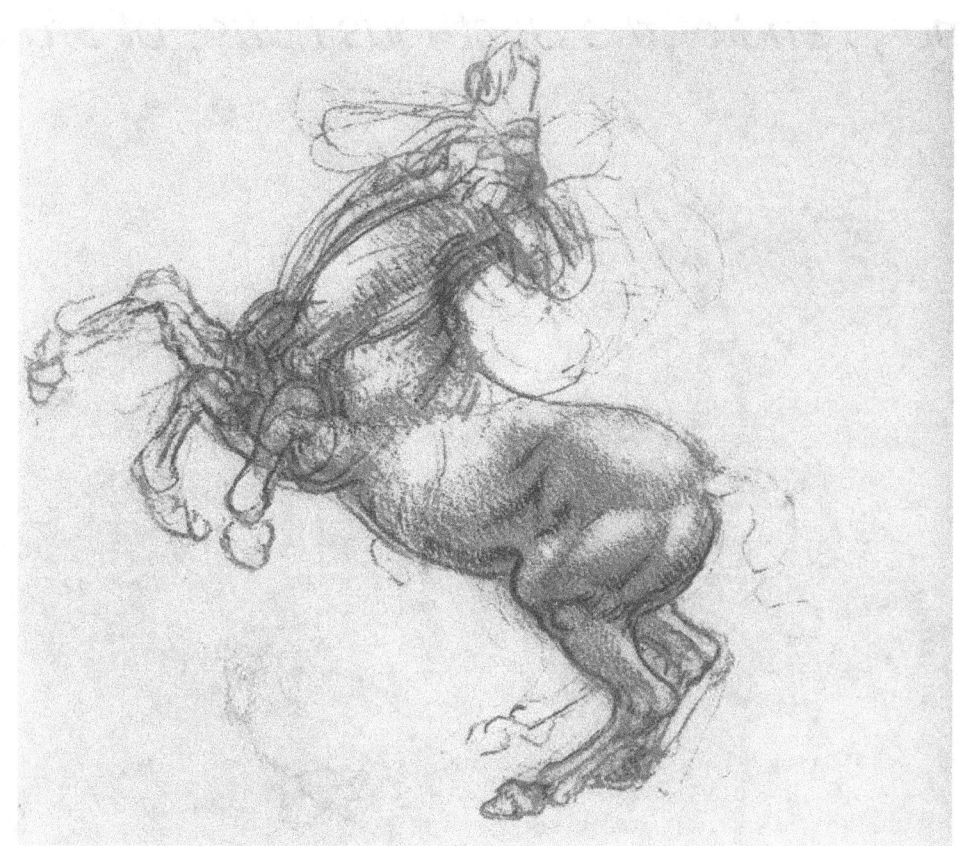

"Of the horse, I shall say nothing, because I know the times."

"Again the bronze horse may be taken in hand, which is to be to the immortal glory and eternal honour of the prince your father of happy memory, and of the illustrious house of Sforza."

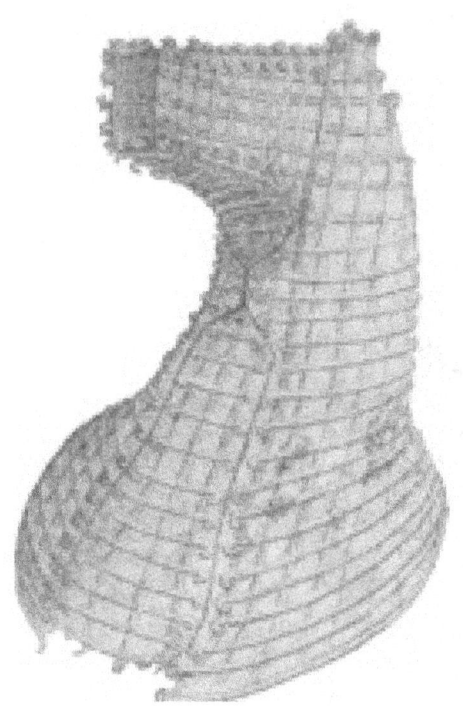

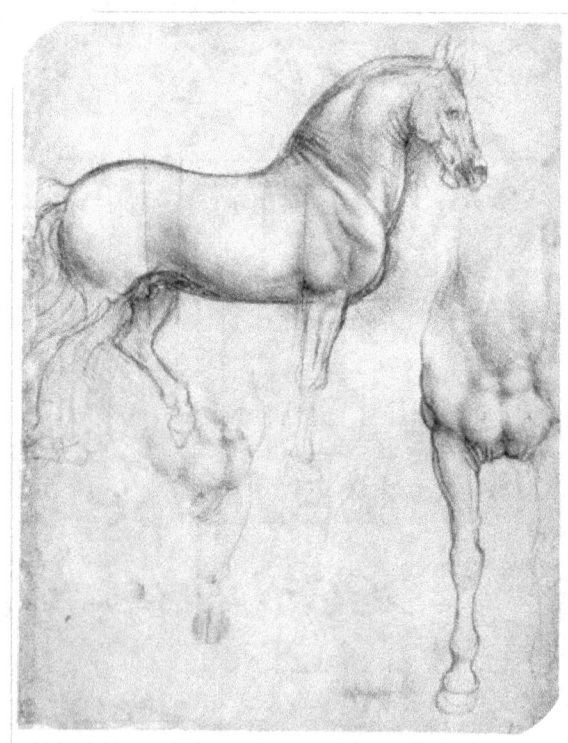

Leonardo's Horse

C	J	J	W	C	Q	V	T	I	S	G	A	J	L	A	I	H
A	H	B	N	N	X	E	X	P	C	N	I	P	E	T	E	B
R	K	A	D	I	K	V	E	I	Z	N	K	F	A	W	R	L
D	I	U	R	Y	N	D	T	V	P	S	I	L	T	V	U	D
X	K	J	L	L	E	A	T	S	U	P	Y	V	G	L	T	M
E	T	P	T	S	E	O	A	R	I	H	Q	B	A	G	P	O
S	K	E	T	C	H	S	X	K	E	T	R	E	S	D	L	N
B	M	A	N	K	V	U	D	U	A	O	R	Y	J	S	U	U
E	L	M	I	L	A	N	T	E	N	M	X	A	H	I	C	M
N	A	W	H	I	M	A	Y	Z	N	K	U	C	W	E	S	E
M	P	C	K	R	T	O	E	X	Z	T	N	H	R	E	W	N
M	A	T	L	S	Q	J	L	I	J	E	C	O	L	Z	Z	T
U	O	Y	A	L	C	A	P	D	R	L	U	R	E	X	I	W
U	J	D	D	C	F	D	D	F	J	Y	O	S	F	L	B	O
I	C	L	E	P	S	E	L	C	S	U	M	E	W	R	K	T
M	T	R	Z	L	E	Z	K	R	K	L	U	Q	T	A	J	Z

1. Statue
2. Gift
3. Sculpture
4. Bronze
5. Muscles
6. Pedestal
7. Clay
8. Model
9. Charles Dent

10. Sketch
11. Duke
12. Monument
13. Milan
14. Mold
15. Nina Akamu
16. Italy
17. Artist
18. Da Vinci

Student Activity:

After sketching horses, we worked on our own Horse Sculptures, using modeling clay, toothpicks, pipe cleaners, straws, and popsicle sticks.

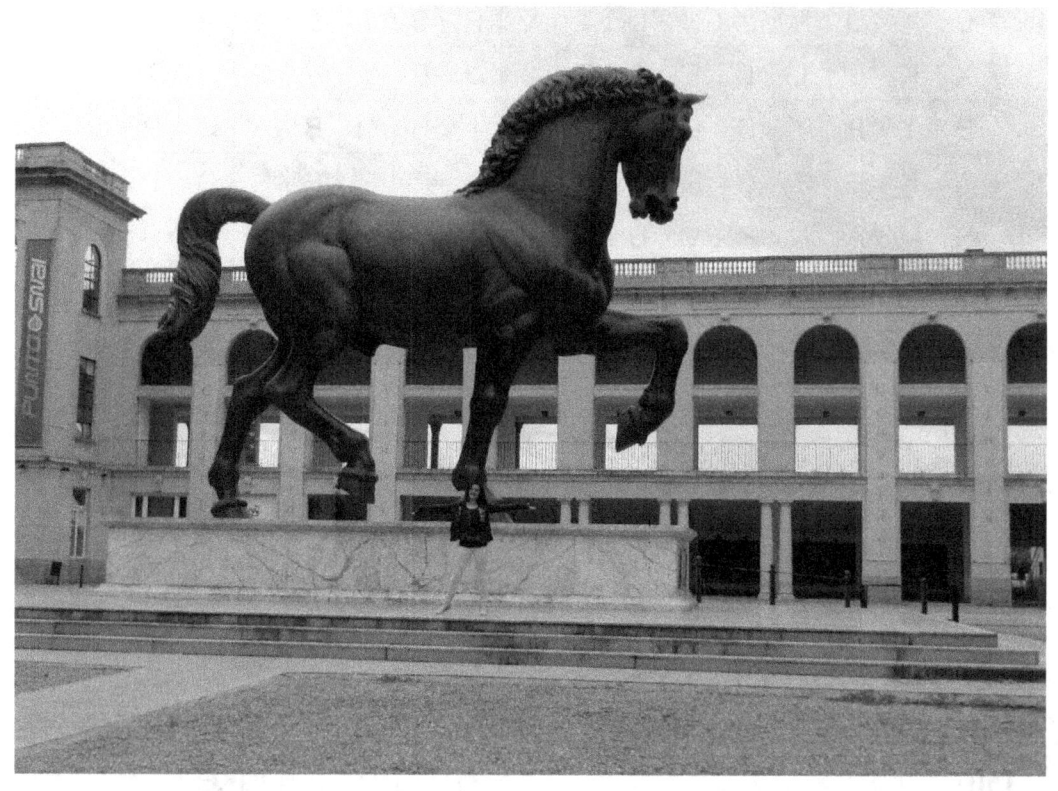

The Horse Sculpture in Milan, Italy

Duke Lodovico liked the idea of a monument with a horse and rider representing his father, the soldier-hero. When Leonardo wrote Lodovico his extensive letter/resume, it was as if what Leonardo *wanted* to do was more important in his own mind than what he had already done. And Leonardo mentioned the horse project almost in passing at the end of his letter to the duke.

Leonardo had some experience in this area; he had helped his master, Andrea del Verrocchio, in his research for an equestrian statue. (Verrocchio in Venice in 1488, and Donatello in Padua in 1453, had both completed equestrian monuments to military heroes, both of which Leonardo would have been familiar with.)

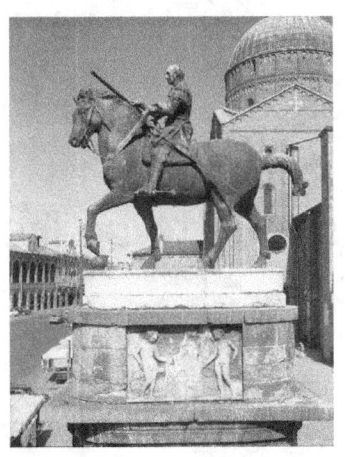 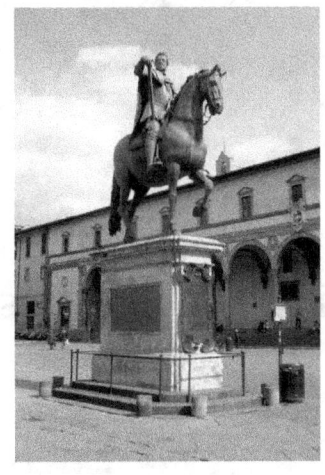

Similar monuments – in Padua and Florence

The Duke never answered Leonardo's letter, but Leonardo moved to Milan the next year, when he was about 30-years-old, and there received the title of "painter and engineer of the duke." The Duke most likely hired him specifically to build the statue, which da Vinci eventually worked in among his other projects. It was an interesting assignment for Leonardo to even contemplate —he considered sculpting to be much inferior to painting!

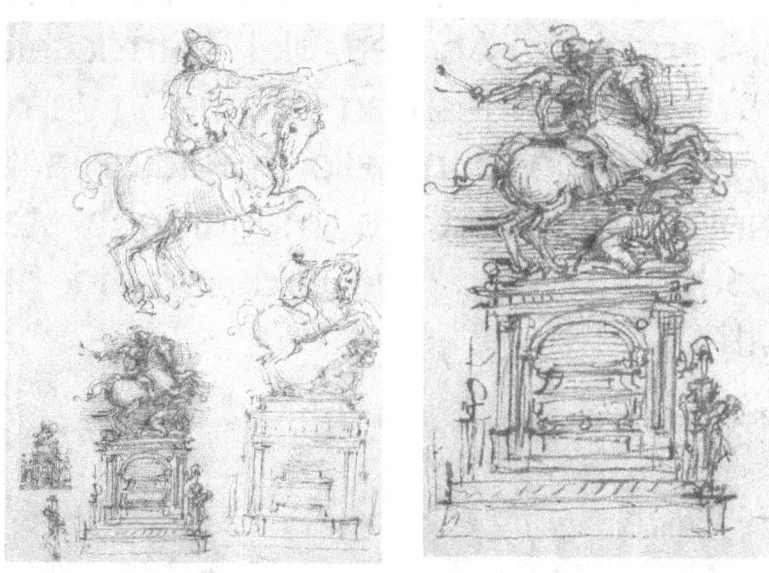

Original plans called for the statue to be life-size, with the horse in a rearing position.

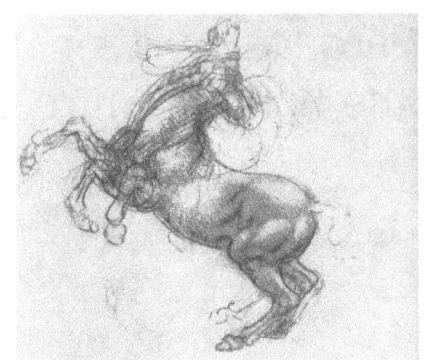

While working on *The Last Supper*, Leonardo would also work on his horse sculpture. As with his other projects, Leonardo could not be rushed. He spent years studying horses, even dissecting a few to make sure he understood how their muscles worked together.

He also spent years on the design for the monument, visiting many other similar statues in the area. His had to be better than all the others! Of course, by 1485, three years after hiring Leonardo, the Duke was getting impatient to have his monument completed, and by 1489 he was actually looking for another artist to take over the project.

It didn't help that over time the Duke had also changed his mind about what he wanted: He decided his statue should be four times life-size, which would have made it the largest monument of its kind in that day. The horse was now to be twenty-four feet tall. To accommodate the larger size, Leonardo had to change the positioning of the horse from rearing to standing.

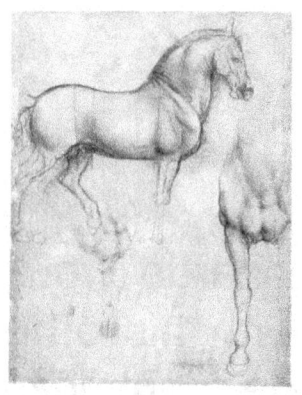 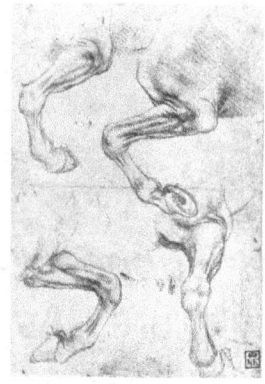 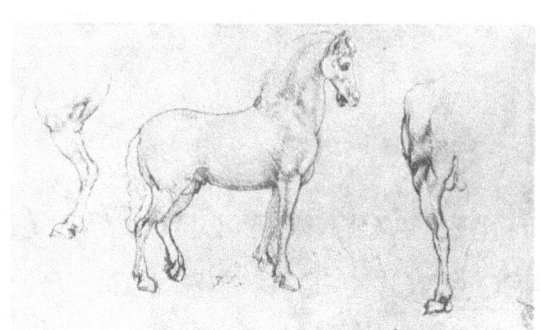

He also worked hard to develop a new system for casting the statue, so it could be cast in one piece; something that had never been done for a statue of this size.

Leonardo did not want to use the current system of "lost wax" casting, which caused a number of problems, including that the mold was never reusable in this method.[9] He invented a new way to use a double mold to make the cast. He took extensive notes in his notebooks of his various plans for the statue.

───────────────

[9] *In the "lost-wax" method, a model was made out of wax, the mold would be made over the wax – and then the wax was melted out and replaced with bronze.*

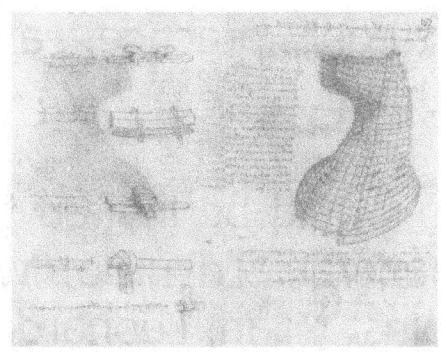

And he planned to cast the horse upside down, to resolve some of the problems with the weight in a statue of this size.

By 1493, just in time for the wedding of Bianca Sforza, daughter of the Duke of Milan, and Emperor Maximilian, Leonardo unveiled a twenty-four feet tall clay model of the horse. It was beautiful, and people came from miles away to gaze at it. In 1494 he finally began preparing the molds for the actual statue.

The amount of metal needed to cast was tremendous, about eighty tons, and Leonardo worked to collect it while he "perfected" his design and technique. Unfortunately, Milan was attacked by France in 1499 and had to use the collected metal for cannon balls.

Milan still lost the battle with the French, the Duke fled, and so did Leonardo. The French archers used his huge clay horse for target practice, and it eventually crumbled into nothing.

In 1508 Leonardo would be invited to make a statue for the Italian general, Trivulzio, who had led the French troops against Milan. Leonardo actually worked on plans for it, but that statue was never completed either.

Leonardo would lament the unfinished horse for the rest of his life: *"Of the horse, I shall say nothing, because I know the times."*

In 1966, 467 years after the French invasion halted the equine project, sketches of Leonardo da Vinci's horse were rediscovered in Spain. And in 1977 *National Geographic* ran a very short piece about "The Horse That Never Was." Charles Dent, a United Airlines pilot, read the article, and became very interested in finally building Leonardo's horse as a gift to Italy.

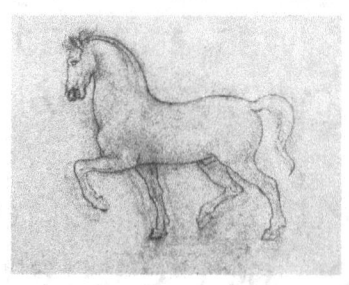

And on September 10, 1999, exactly five hundred years after the soldiers had destroyed Leonardo's clay model, Charles Dent and Leonardo da Vinci's dream horse was unveiled in Milan, Italy. [10] Nina Akamu had completed their project. *The Horse* stands proudly there on a marble pedestal.[11]

With the help of many others, Da Vinci's promise to the Duke had finally been fulfilled:

> "10. *In time of peace I believe I can carry out sculpture in marble, bronze, or clay, and also in painting whatever may be done, and as well as any other, be he whom he may... Again the bronze horse may be taken in hand, which is to be to the immortal glory and eternal honour of the prince your father of happy memory...*"

And so, Leonardo's "Horse That Never Was" finally *is*, in multiple places!

---

[10] *Total costs for the project exceeded $4 million. Pictures of the statue in Milan can be seen at:*
http://www.leonardoshorse.org/site.asp
[11] *Jean Fritz wrote a great children's book,* Leonardo's Horse, *about both Leonardo's work on the horse, and Dent's project almost 500 years later.*

Travel Years – Overview:

When Duke Ludovico lost Milan to the French in 1499, Leonardo left the city searching for new employment. He would spend much of the next six years wandering across Italy, during which time he did very little artistic work, but a significant amount of scientific work. He traveled first to Vaprio and Mantua, then on to Venice, and eventually he returned to Florence for a brief stay.

In 1502, he took one of his most unusual assignments, working for the military dictator, Cesare Borgia, for almost a year, traveling throughout the region of Romagna during much of that time. That same year, he submitted plans to the Ottoman Sultan for a bridge the Sultan wanted to build over the mouth of the Black Sea.

When Leonardo tired of his work as a military advisor, he took a commission in Florence, and returned there a "local hero." During the next few years he traveled between Florence and Milan several times, often in an attempt to settle family issues caused by the lack of a will at his father's death, or a contested will after his uncle's death.

LEONARDO DA VINCI, MILITARY ADVISOR

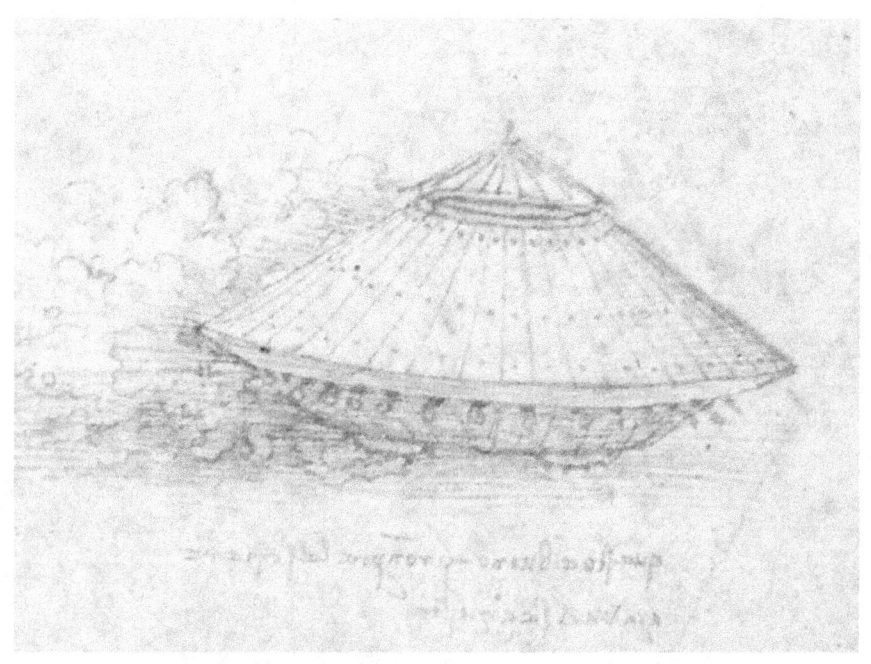

"If by reason of the height of the banks, or the strength of the place and its position, it is impossible, when besieging a place, to avail oneself of the plan of bombardment, I have methods for destroying every rock or other fortress, even if it were founded on a rock, etc."

"If the fortress can be attacked only from a single side, make that side in the form of a massive acute angle of 25 – 30 feet, with its lateral defenses..."

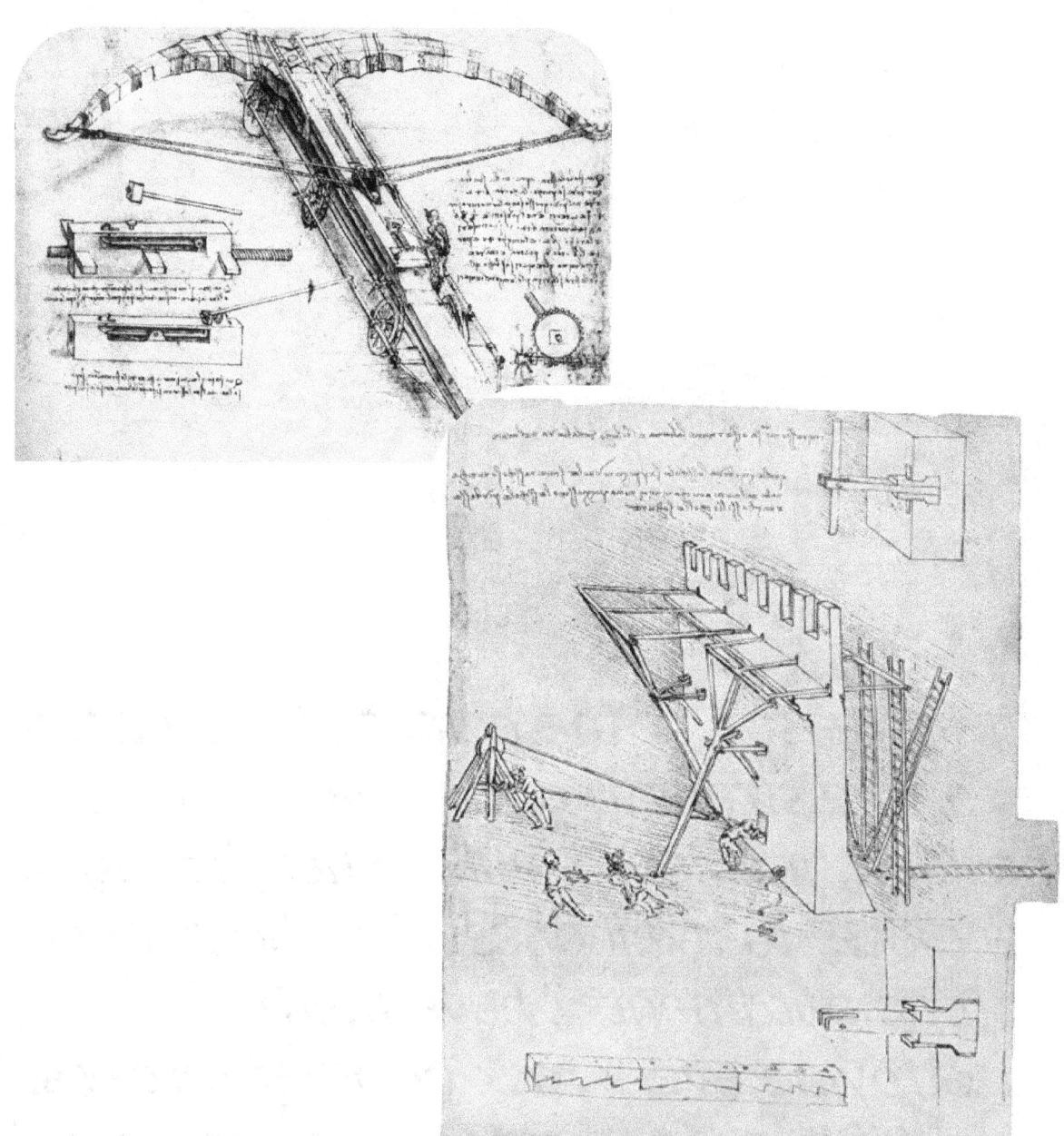

Leonardo's Work as a Military Advisor

U	H	U	F	L	Y	I	N	G	S	H	I	P	F	S	E	N
E	R	A	R	O	N	U	G	E	N	I	H	C	A	M	D	O
X	N	O	N	A	N	G	J	P	R	X	H	N	O	I	N	G
T	L	Z	S	G	X	A	A	Y	Z	L	V	K	V	E	I	A
K	B	G	D	J	G	R	V	G	T	U	I	I	N	R	D	W
E	X	Y	E	Z	A	L	R	A	D	K	N	X	E	A	D	S
H	N	K	T	C	J	P	I	P	L	G	B	T	G	U	T	S
A	J	I	H	S	G	G	U	D	B	C	P	F	Z	O	N	E
K	J	U	R	Y	F	C	E	A	E	O	A	Z	Z	N	D	L
O	T	Y	R	A	O	X	L	F	C	R	C	N	C	C	N	E
E	U	B	I	Y	M	L	N	I	P	B	Y	A	N	N	X	S
O	A	F	Z	D	Z	B	L	O	P	S	J	N	X	O	M	R
A	R	E	R	A	G	E	U	W	K	N	C	O	Z	Z	N	O
D	L	P	P	B	H	P	W	S	C	C	E	Y	N	J	F	H
T	O	Z	F	O	B	P	O	N	T	O	O	N	B	O	A	T
X	H	S	O	T	I	U	S	G	N	I	V	I	D	W	Q	Q

1. Tank
2. Hang Glider
3. Horseless Wagon
4. Pontoon Boat
5. Helicopter
6. Parachute

7. Machine Gun
8. Diving Suit
9. Submarine
10. Flying Ship
11. Naval Cannon

Where Did Leonardo Work as a Military Advisor?

C	M	M	X	Z	S	Q	A	R	N	R	W	N	H	K	S	F
S	E	R	R	A	V	A	L	L	E	M	T	N	P	A	S	S
A	H	G	K	J	W	D	E	Y	O	T	T	A	M	Q	Z	O
C	B	E	U	R	O	I	P	Y	P	M	D	N	U	Y	W	Q
W	Z	C	R	S	J	L	D	N	L	G	I	G	L	D	Q	Z
D	P	B	B	C	G	H	W	B	Y	N	O	A	D	R	P	M
I	E	C	I	H	E	Q	L	N	X	H	T	M	I	J	I	V
G	S	F	N	L	S	S	P	Q	R	I	J	O	T	L	O	N
F	A	R	O	H	O	H	E	E	I	S	P	R	M	C	M	M
L	R	A	G	V	L	B	V	N	M	E	L	A	X	I	B	D
O	O	T	N	L	C	I	J	L	A	O	C	J	T	N	I	Y
R	R	X	P	D	R	A	F	W	X	A	K	U	Y	A	N	R
E	M	W	C	O	L	R	A	I	N	I	M	I	R	L	O	T
N	J	V	N	G	J	W	G	C	O	J	U	T	C	I	O	Y
C	E	R	I	N	M	R	V	O	F	J	G	Q	X	M	M	P
E	A	B	S	E	K	C	N	I	O	E	V	Z	D	F	T	L

1. Piombino	6. Arno River
2. Pesaro	7. Florence
3. Milan	8. Imola
4. Cesena	9. Rimini
5. Romagna	10. Urbino

Student Activity:

After sketching a variety of military ideas, we worked on our own designs/models of catapults and trebuchets using cardboard, cardboard rolls, plastic spoons, rubber bands, and tape.

We also enjoyed portions of Nova's video: *Medieval Siege* from the Secrets of Lost Empires series. It shows two groups designing and testing different trebuchets based on medieval designs.

Leonardo made a practice of always carrying a small notebook with him and then copying his notes, sketches, etc. onto larger sheets each evening. His notebooks were generally unorganized, usually consisting of loose pages, that he only occasionally bound himself. They included notes on countless things, including ideas for weapons.

Even though Leonardo hated war, and considered himself a pacifist, many of his ideas were for tools useful in military operations:

- Diving Bell
- Diving Suit
- Flying Ship
- Hang Glider
- Helicopter
- Horseless Wagon
- Machine Gun
- Naval Cannon
- Parachute
- Pontoon Bridges
- Revolving Bridge
- Submarine
- Tank
- Temporary Bridges
    to name "a few"...

In fact, when Leonardo was looking for a job with Duke Lodovico, he emphasized his ideas for offensive and defensive war machines more than his artistic abilities.

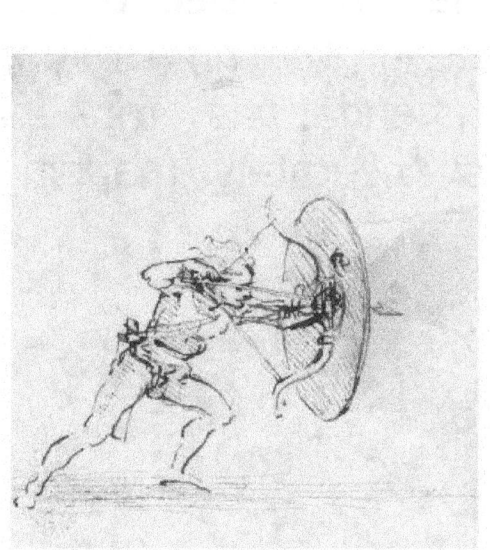 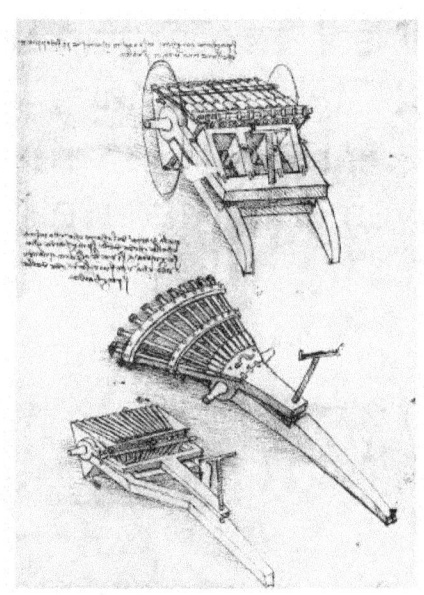

From 1499 – 1502, Cesare Borgia, military dictator, was ruthless in his attempt to gain power over Romagna, a central portion of Italy. He was encouraged in his efforts by his father, Pope Alexander VI.

In 1502, Leonardo took one of his most unusual assignments, working for Cesare Borgia, as "senior military architect and general engineer" for almost a year. During that time he met Niccolo Machiavelli, who was also working for Borgia. (Many years later

Machiavelli would write his most famous book, *The Prince*, significantly based on the unscrupulous means by which Borgia conquered and ruled.)

As advisor to Borgia, Leonardo traveled throughout central Italy — Imola, Cesena, Rimini, Urbino, and Pesaro. He gave recommendations for military improvements, as well as accurately mapping the region.

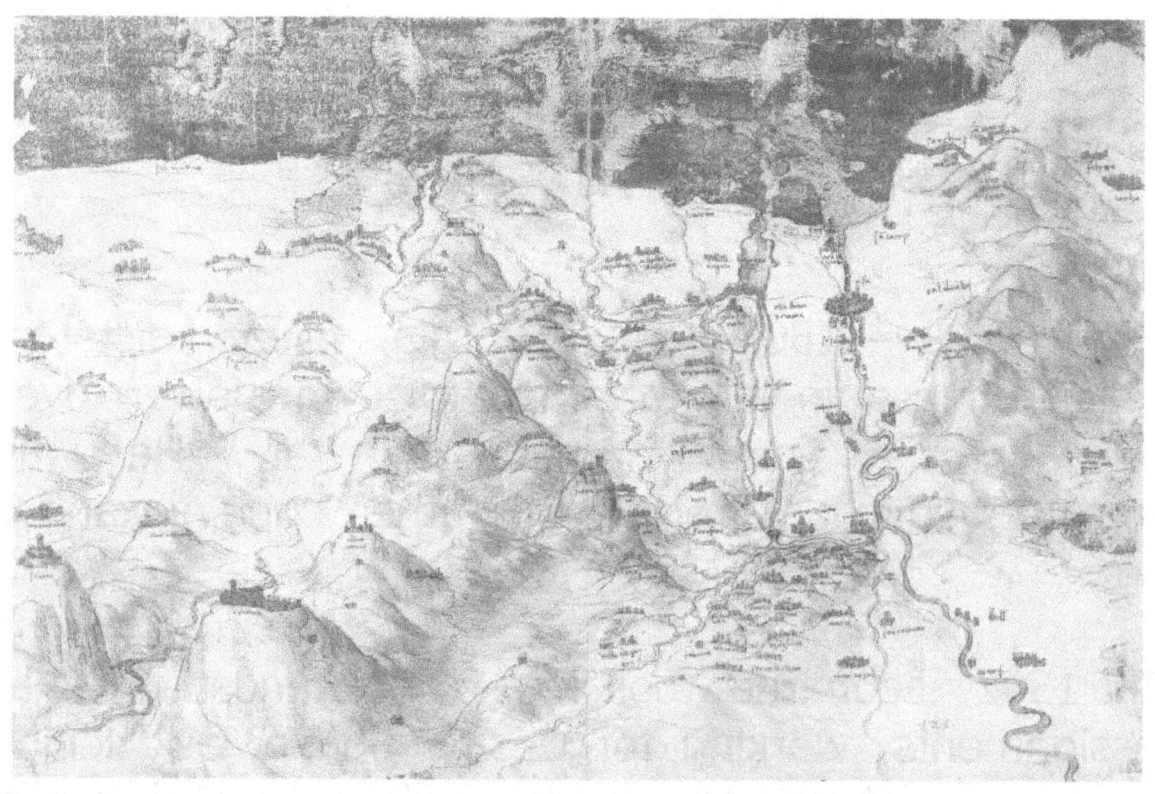

Leonardo's Map of Tuscany

Later da Vinci was in Piombino to improve the fortifications of the town Borgia had just taken from Jacopo Appiani.

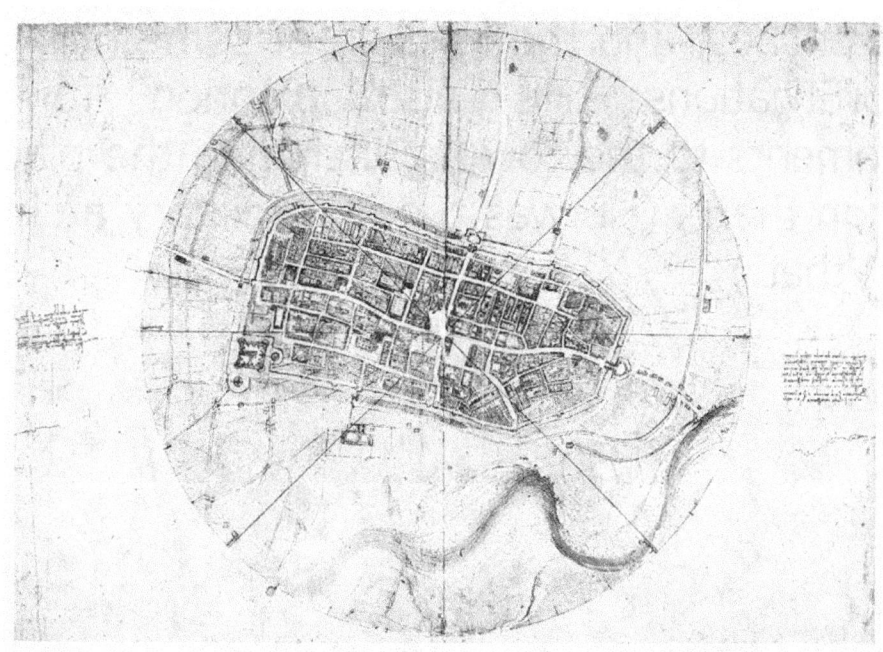

Map of Imola created by da Vinci for Cesare Borgia

Back in Florence, Leonardo worked with Machiavelli for over a year trying to divert the Arno River with canals, for military and transportation purposes. It would have involved tunneling through the Serravalle Mountain Pass.[12]

---

[12] *The tunneling and canals were finally done in modern times, and Leonardo's exact route was used.*

After the downfall of Borgia, Leonardo went back to Piombino briefly. Here Machiavelli was attempting a diplomatic mission, when Leonardo came to advise the new/old leader, Appiani, on the city's fortifications. Leonardo's recommendations included a tunnel or moat, trenches, and the leveling of some hills outside the fortifications. He also planned for some improvements to the towers, including the placement of cannon there. (He was the first military architect to suggest that.)

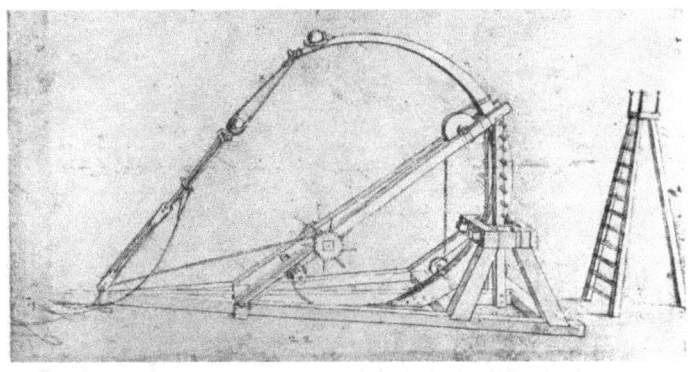

For a man who despised war, Leonardo spent much time advising those who practiced it![13]

---

[13] *Possibly out of a false sense of loyalty, but more likely for the money – since he frequently needed to worry about who his next patron would be.*

LEONARDO DA VINCI'S BRIDGE(S)

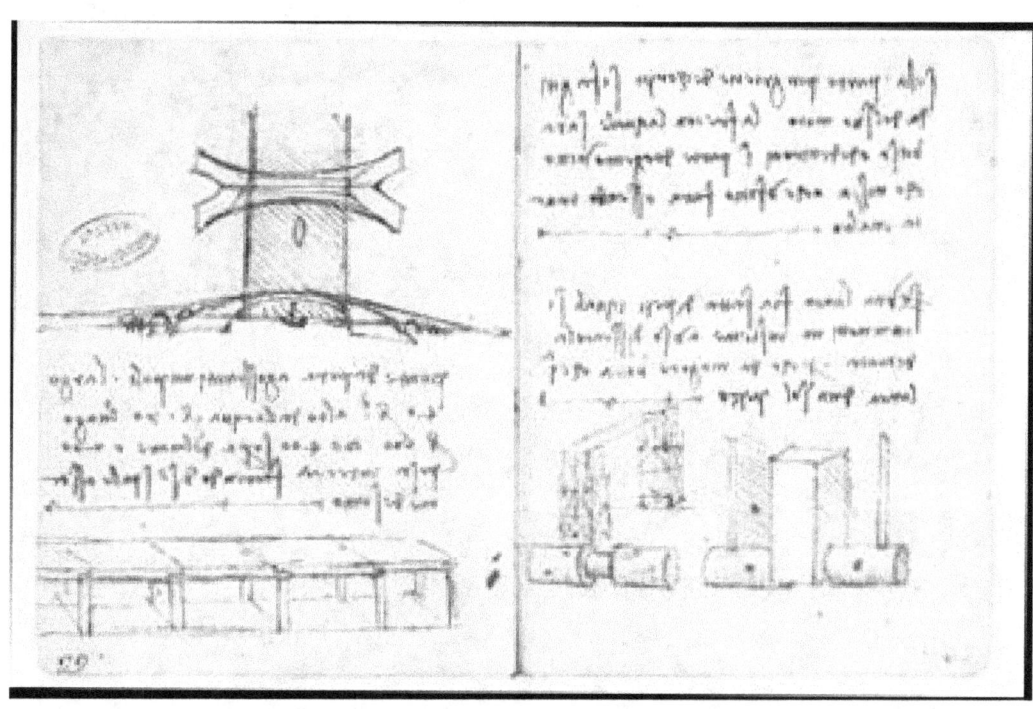

"I have plans for bridges"

"I have a sort of extremely light and strong bridges, adapted to be most easily carried..."

Top View →

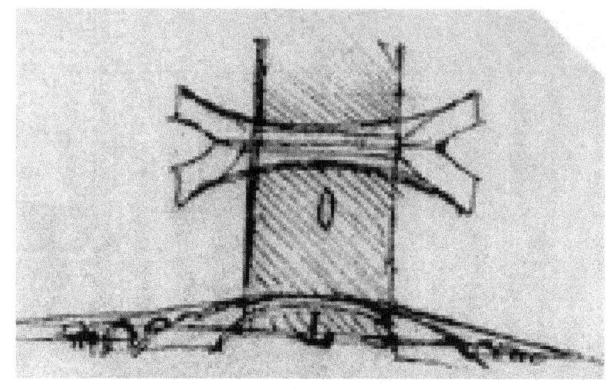

Side View →

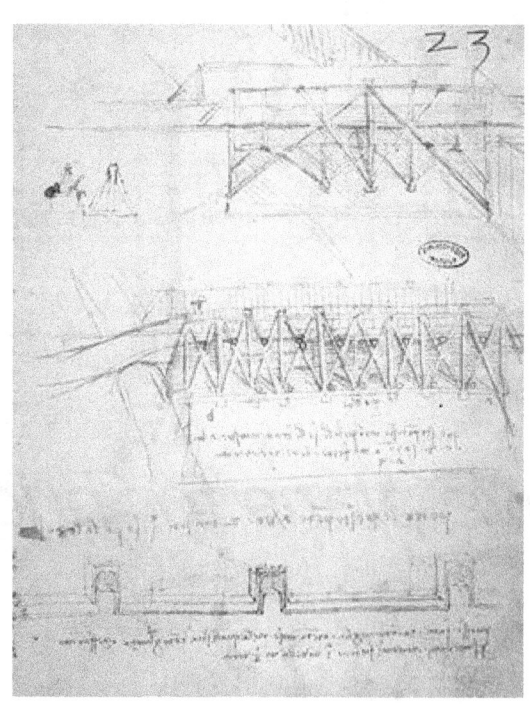

Leonardo's Bridge

I	I	M	R	U	Y	E	Q	M	U	Z	A	L	A	J	X	Q
S	U	L	T	A	N	B	A	J	A	Z	E	T	I	I	V	T
N	S	D	W	J	S	F	Z	C	Y	P	X	E	G	E	X	F
K	F	R	N	E	M	I	C	H	E	L	A	N	G	E	L	O
M	O	Q	H	A	W	Y	N	O	I	S	N	E	P	S	U	S
N	H	C	B	S	S	R	U	I	H	Z	T	U	Z	X	G	T
U	R	K	I	O	A	M	R	U	L	D	E	V	A	U	H	I
A	Q	J	R	A	R	G	O	L	D	E	N	H	O	R	N	M
G	D	E	G	P	F	G	Y	J	Q	T	C	J	G	N	A	B
D	A	O	A	Q	A	U	I	R	B	W	C	K	L	S	F	E
L	V	R	I	T	D	W	G	A	U	E	Z	V	D	D	Y	R
A	I	N	C	U	J	X	B	Z	Y	A	V	N	L	F	M	T
M	N	W	E	R	I	P	M	E	N	A	M	O	T	T	O	R
M	C	P	U	C	I	L	C	Y	E	G	D	I	R	B	V	U
E	I	A	J	N	O	S	N	E	E	U	Q	R	B	H	R	S
T	I	M	B	E	R	C	A	N	T	I	L	E	V	E	R	S

1. Golden Horn
2. Ottoman Empire
3. Suspension
4. Da Vinci
5. Bridge
6. Timber Truss
7. Arches
8. Michelangelo
9. Borgia
10. Norway
11. Sultan Bajazet II
12. Queen Sonja
13. Timber Cantilever
14. Vebjorn Sand

Student Activities:

First, we studied the different architectural styles of bridges through the ages, comparing and contrasting them.

Then we sketched bridges on our own, and then worked on our bridge models, using cardboard, paper, straws, toothpicks, and popsicle sticks.

In addition to his artwork, which he was so famous for, Leonardo spent much of his time on various types of design work. His designs included bridges at different times in his career, including when he wrote his letter/resume to the Duke of Milan. The first portion of the letter, where he refers to bridges is included below:

To My Lord the Duke of Milan,
Florence, 1482

Most Illustrious Lord,

Having until now sufficiently considered the specimens of all those who proclaim themselves skilled contrivers of instruments of war, and that the invention and operation of the said instruments are nothing different to those in common use: I shall endeavor, without prejudice to any one else, to explain myself to your Excellency showing your Lordship my secrets, and then offering them to your best pleasure and approbation to work with effect at opportune moments as well as all those things which in part, shall be briefly noted below:

> 1. *I have a sort of extremely light and strong bridges, adapted to be most easily carried, and with them you may pursue, and at any time flee from the enemy; and others, secure*

and indestructible by fire and battle, easy and convenient to lift and place. Also methods to burn and destroy those of the enemy.

I know how, when a place is besieged, to take the water out of the trenches, and make endless variety of <u>bridges</u>, and covered ways and ladders, and other machines pertaining to such expeditions.

His notebooks included designs for a Swing Bridge, a Retractable Bridge, and a Self-Supporting Bridge.

Leonardo was offered another unique assignment while working for Cesare Borgia. This time it was Sultan Bajazet II, ruler of the Ottoman Empire, who considered hiring him.

The Sultan had sent ambassadors to the region of Italy to find engineers to design a bridge over the Bosphorus, or Golden Horn, at the mouth of the Black Sea. Leonardo drew up plans for the Sultan's bridge, shown on the next page. The Sultan and his advisors thought Leonardo's bridge, a giant arch shape, [14] was

---

[14] *You have to look closely at the bottom portion of the drawing to see the arch shape.*

too radical, and that it would not be strong enough in the middle.[15]

Leonardo was so convinced of his design that he offered to build the bridge himself. Instead, the Sultan requested that Leonardo's rival, Michelangelo, submit an alternate set of plans, but Michelangelo was busy in Rome, and declined the offer. The Sultan never got his bridge built – and bridges were not built across the Golden Horn for over 300 years – until 1836 and 1845.

Leonardo's bridge was forgotten about for many centuries until a Norwegian artist saw the plans at a Leonardo da Vinci exhibit in 1996, and fell in love with Leonardo's idea.

The Norwegian artist, Vebjorn Sand, convinced the Norwegian Highway Department to build a scaled down version of the bridge. In 2002, Norwegian Queen Sonja, unveiled the beautiful arch bridge, designed 500 years earlier by Leonardo da Vinci.[16] Sand now hopes to build one of the bridges on every continent.

---

[15] *Had it been built, at almost 1100 feet in length, it would have been the longest bridge of its day.*
[16] *Pictures of the bridge in Norway can be seen at*
http://www.vebjorn-sand.com/thebridge.htm

Other arch bridges throughout the ages, and throughout the world, have included:

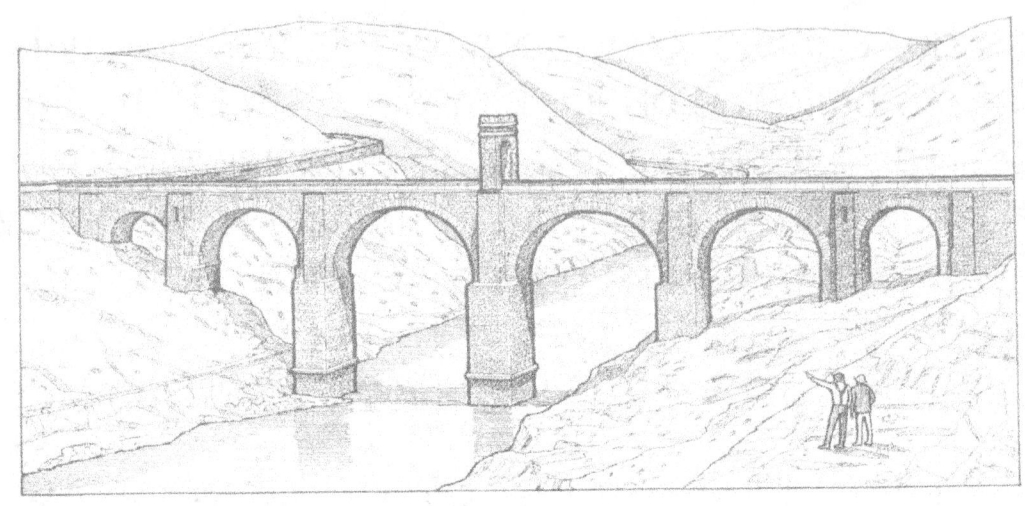

Puente Alcantara, *a Roman stone-arch bridge in Spain from the 1st Century.*

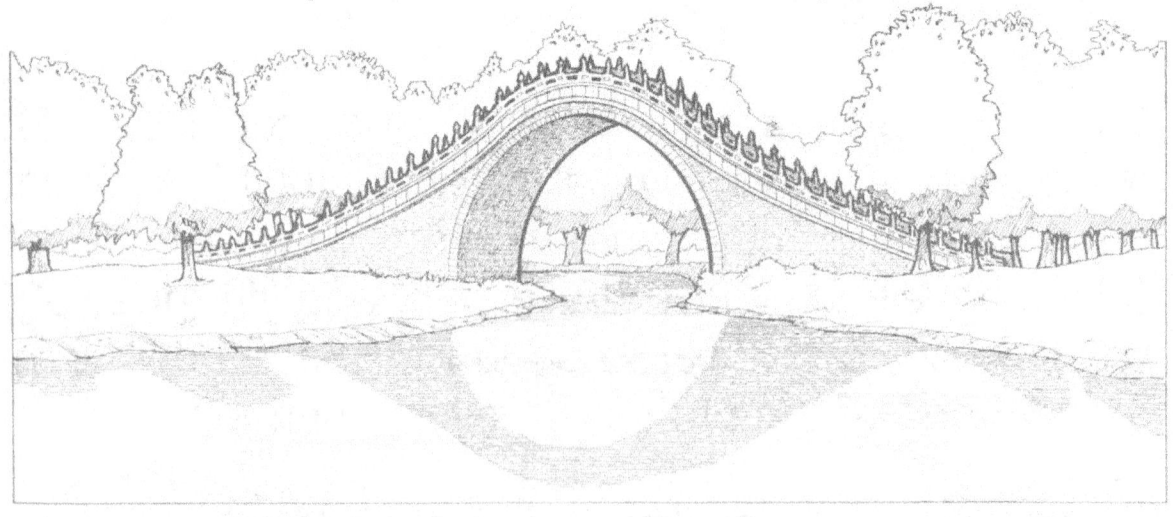

This **Chinese Camel-Back Arched Bridge** *from the 12th century.*

Other popular bridge styles have included:

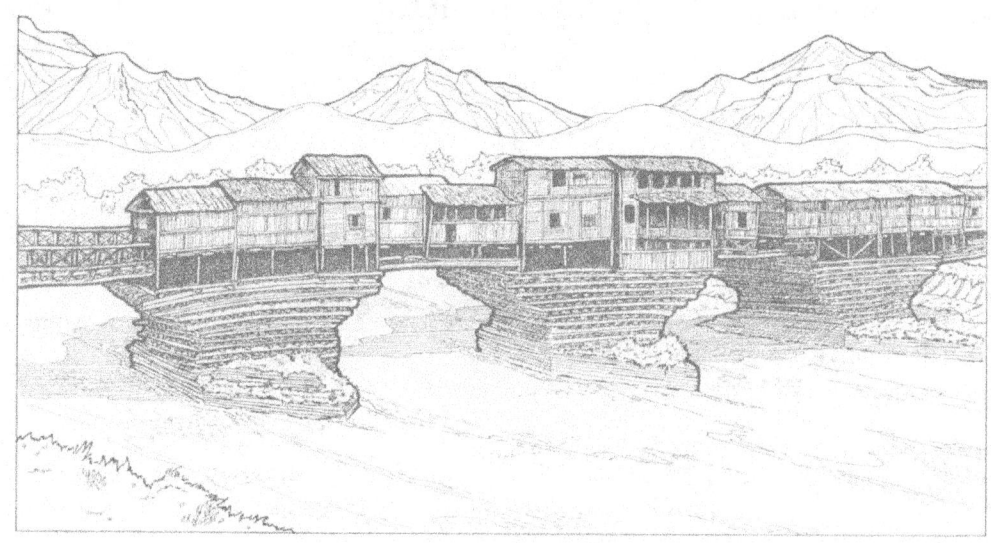

*This **timber cantilever bridge** in India was constructed during the 19th century.*

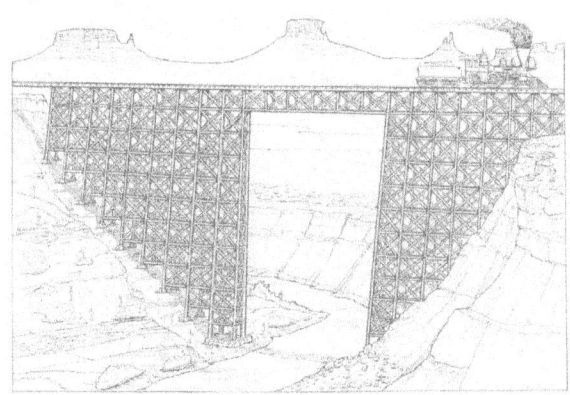

*This **timber-truss railroad bridge** was a popular bridge type in the westward expansion of the United States during the same time period, the late 19th century.*

Modern bridges are often suspension bridges. Two famous examples of those include:

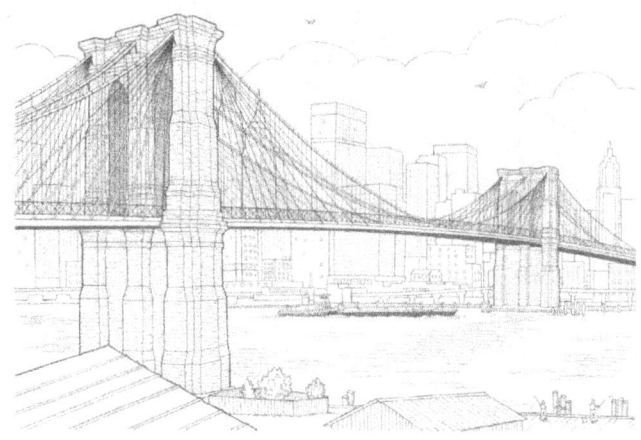

The Brooklyn Bridge *in New York City, was the longest suspension bridge in the world when it was completed in 1883.*

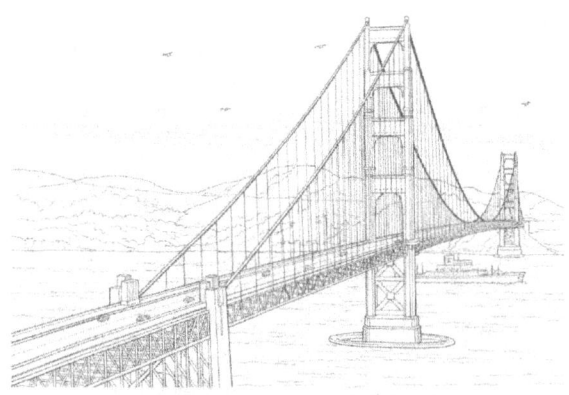

The Golden Gate Bridge *in San Francisco, was the longest suspension bridge in the world when it was completed in 1937.*

LEONARDO DA VINCI AND FLIGHT

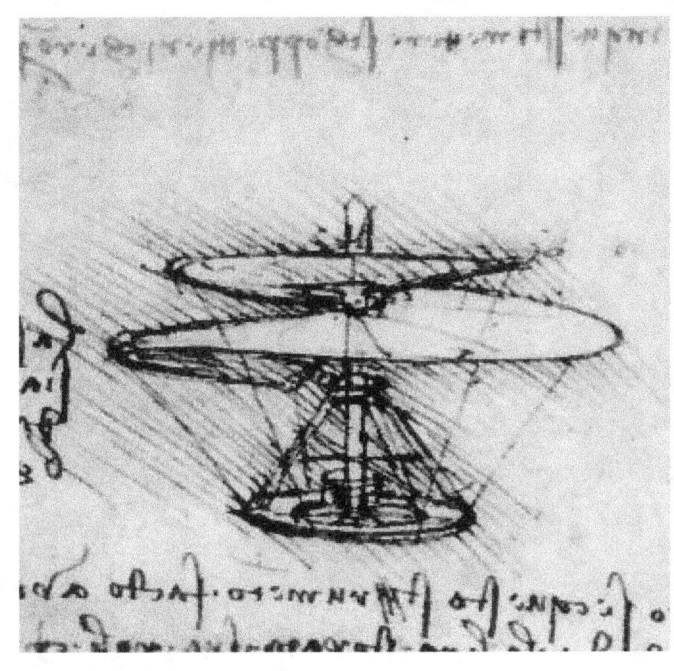

"When once you have tasted flight, you will forever walk the earth with your eyes turned skyward, for there you have been, and there you will always long to return."

"Feathers shall raise men even as they do birds..."

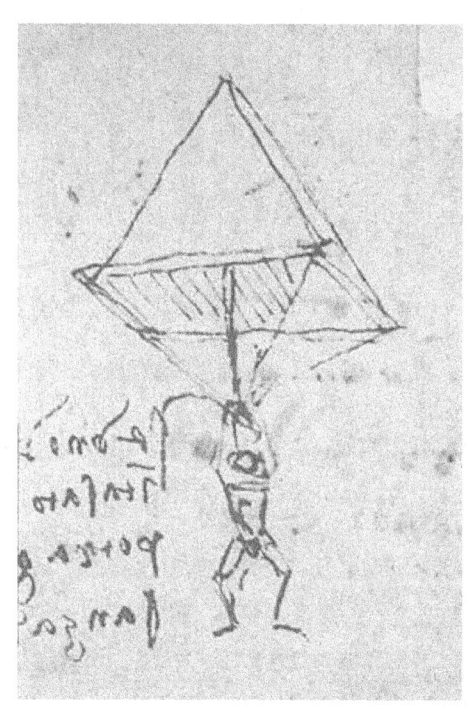

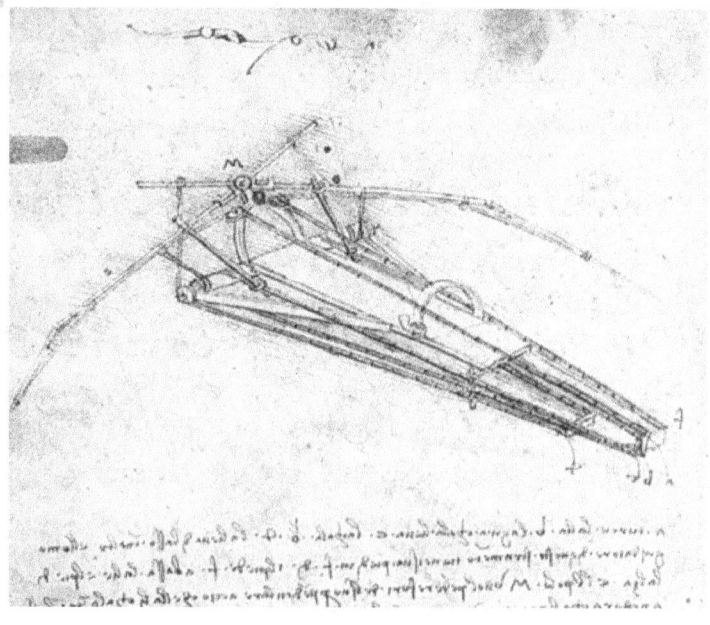

Leonardo's Flight

X	F	E	R	J	Z	R	S	N	B	F	R	H	O	U	R	E
O	L	F	T	T	X	G	D	B	H	E	M	H	K	E	M	X
R	Y	E	V	U	Y	B	R	K	T	C	E	T	E	A	Z	R
N	I	M	C	F	H	J	Y	P	D	A	V	I	N	C	I	M
I	N	S	L	N	I	C	O	Z	W	M	X	G	G	D	X	M
T	G	V	S	M	A	C	A	G	M	X	O	H	S	P	O	K
H	M	N	C	P	I	T	W	R	Q	M	W	O	X	Z	F	B
O	A	K	M	L	C	X	S	Z	A	I	S	T	H	K	H	D
P	C	P	E	X	N	J	G	I	N	P	K	D	T	Q	R	E
T	H	H	U	K	R	B	I	G	S	L	S	W	R	A	K	Z
E	I	Z	E	T	I	K	S	L	U	E	R	O	W	I	D	U
R	N	U	I	U	E	X	I	W	T	U	R	Y	F	C	B	B
A	E	R	I	A	L	S	C	R	E	W	K	D	X	I	A	Z
W	L	Z	B	N	Y	J	O	I	X	S	Y	U	N	T	Y	M
H	R	E	D	I	L	G	Z	G	K	F	G	F	S	I	C	O
D	C	B	W	U	Y	O	M	V	G	L	Y	O	W	G	W	N

1. Aerial
2. Screw
3. Helicopter
4. Ornithopter
5. Birds
6. Flying Machine
7. Parachute Wings
8. Da Vinci
9. Skyward
10. Glider
11. Wind Resistance
12. Bats
13. Kite

Student Activity:

After sketching flight ideas, the students took their turn at designing parachutes and paper airplanes. For their parachutes, students picked from plastic bags, paper towels, straws, yarn, paperclips, craft sticks, and coffee filters.

Leonardo da Vinci was fascinated by flight, and the idea of humans flying. He spent much time observing birds and bats in flight, analyzing how they flew, and the effects of wind and air resistance on their wings. Leonardo dreamt of developing ways for man to fly.

Leonardo's "Ornithopter":
A Glider Designed so a Human Could Fly with His Own Power

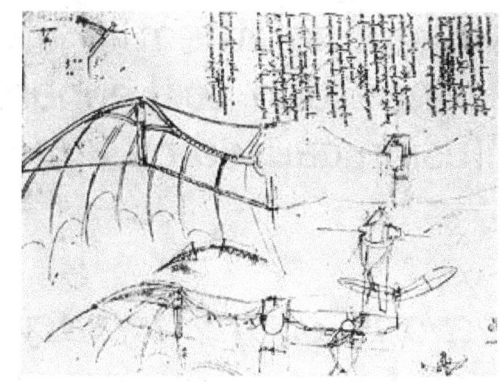

Many of his notebook pages dealing with flight are dated 1505, though some are dated as early as 1483. In 1508 one of his assistants was apparently injured trying out one of Leonardo's flying contraptions.

Leonardo's "Flying Machines"
(It would be another 400 years before successful gliders were built.)

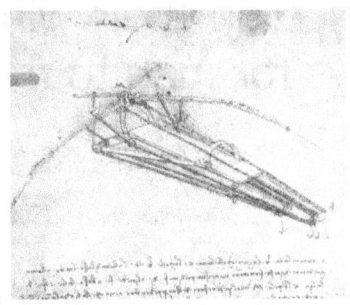 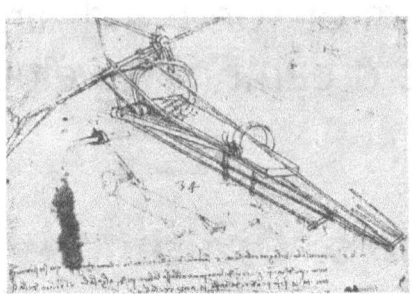

In the East, kites had been in existence almost 1,000 years before Leonardo's day. Sometimes he is mistakenly credited for "inventing" them in the West. There is no proof of a connection to Leonardo, but rather it results from confusion caused by a story from his early childhood:

> *"...among the reflections of my infancy, it seemed to me that, as I was in my cradle, a kite came to me...and struck me several times with its tail..."*

This kite, in his story, was a bird, in the hawk family!

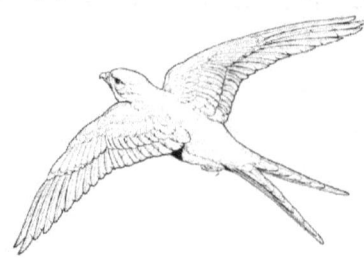

The Aerial Screw
Considered the forerunner to the Helicopter:

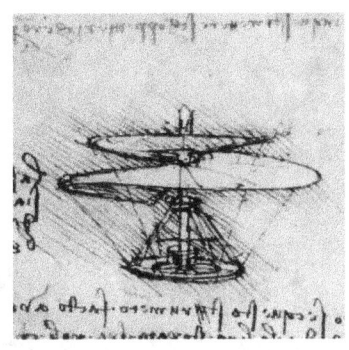

Leonardo said of it:

> "I believe that if this screw device is well manufactured, that is, if it is made of linen cloth, the pores of which have been closed with starch, and if the device is promptly reversed, the screw will engage its gear when in the air and it will rise up on high"

400 years later, shortly after the Wright Brothers had successfully flown their first airplane, a Frenchman flew the first helicopter.

Leonardo's Parachute
The right dimensions, but not the "right shape":

"If a man is provided with a length of gummed linen cloth - linen fabric treated in such a way as to have all interstices filled - with a length of 12 yards on each side and 12 yards high, he can jump from any great height whatsoever, without any injury to his body."

Leonardo da Vinci

Three hundred years later a Frenchman would successfully use a parachute – jumping from a hot air balloon.

And even though he would not live to see men fly, his ideas and designs are often listed first in studies of "the history of flight." Four hundred years after Leonardo da Vinci drew flying contraptions in the pages of his notebooks, the Wright brothers realized his dream of flying.

Leonardo
da Vinci
and
Nature Studies

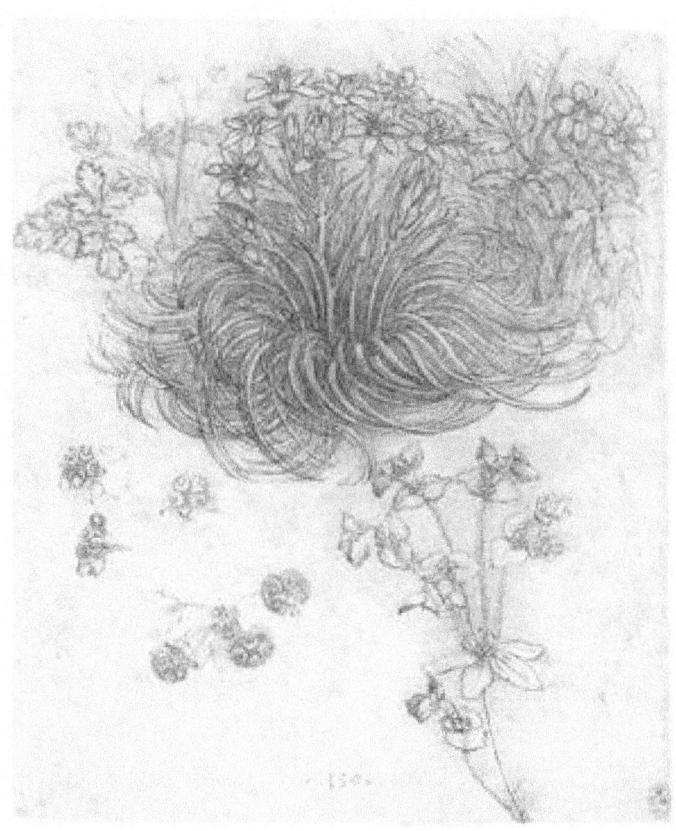

"Consult nature in everything and write it down."

"Human subtlety will never devise an invention more beautiful, more simple or more direct than does nature because in her inventions nothing is lacking, and nothing is superfluous."

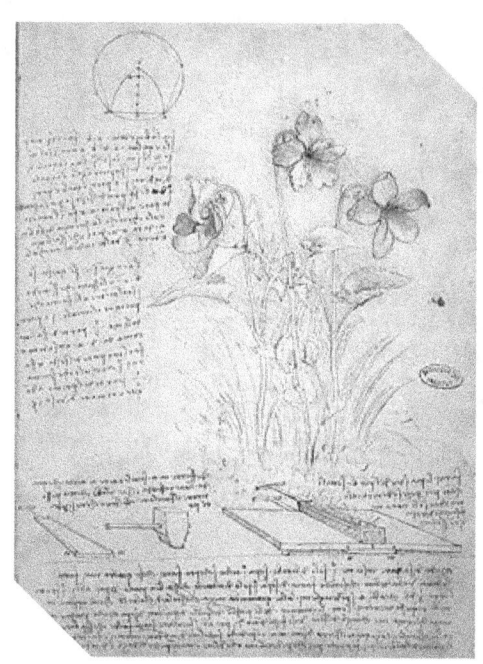
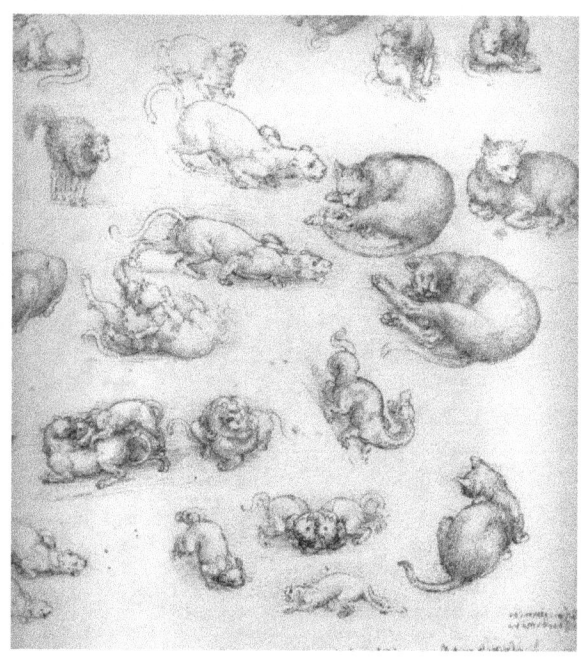

Student Activities:

We started by discussing what Nature is. Leonardo's interest in Nature included Weather, Plants, Animals, and Landscapes.

We read and discussed fables by Leonardo, Aesop, and Rudyard Kipling.

We made sketches of animals and clay models of animals. Some also made habitats for their animals. Students were then encouraged to write an animal poem and/or and animal fables.

In the spirit of Leonardo's observation of plants, we also did leaf rubbings, and sketches of plants.

From Leonardo's youth, he was fascinated by severe weather – tornados, earthquakes, and the like. He did countless drawings showing the effects of severe storms.

"If you wish to represent a tempest, consider its effects as seen and arrange well, when the wind, blowing over the face of the sea and earth, removes and carries with it such things as are not fixed to the general mass."

One of his first drawings was a landscape drawing, which was very unusual for his time period. As he drew he observed: *"Mountains are made by the currents of rivers. Mountains are destroyed by the currents of rivers."*

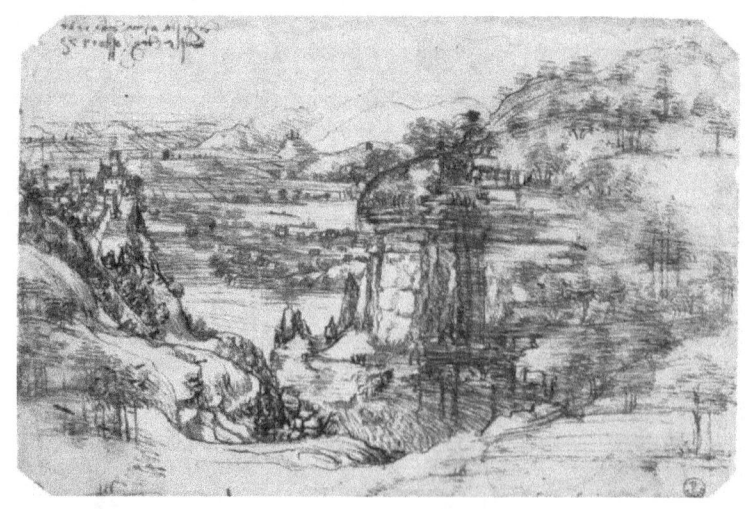

As Leonardo studied all that was around him, he asked:

"Why do we find the bones of great fishes and oysters and corals and various other shells and sea-snails on the high summits of mountains by the sea, just as we find them in low seas?"[17]

As much imagination as Leonardo must have had to do everything he did, his artwork generally came from real life — oftentimes nature. Leonardo also drew many plants in his notebooks, studying the specimens intently as he drew them.

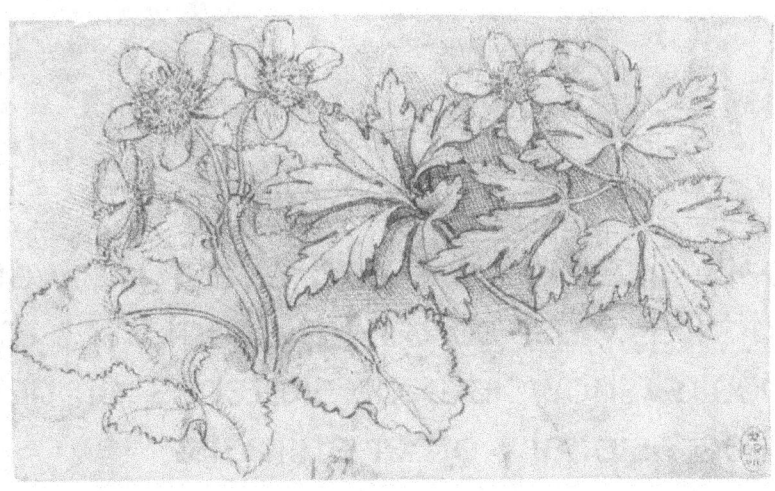

---

[17] *Leonardo didn't believe in Creation, or even "the great flood," but he constantly struggled to get his observations to match his beliefs.*

Botany quickly became another side interest, and Leonardo noted:

> "A leaf always turns its upper side towards the sky so that it may better receive, on all its surface, the dew which drops gently from the atmosphere."

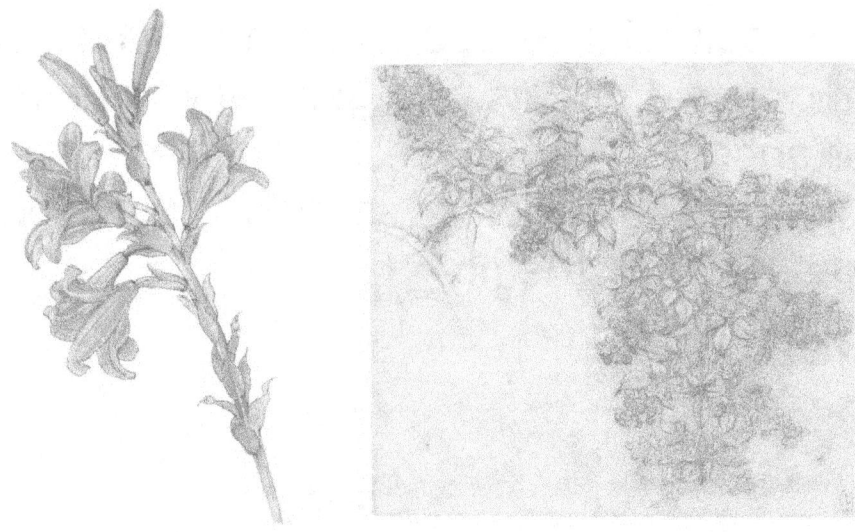

He especially liked horses and birds. He would often buy caged birds, just so that he could set them free. His notebooks show lots of sketches of horses and birds, and occasionally other animals.

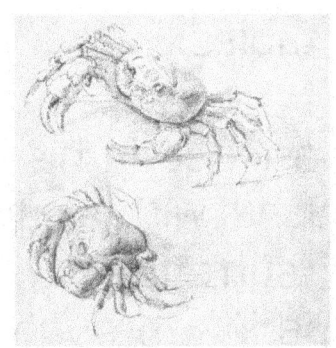

In fact, Leonardo liked animals so much that he became a vegetarian, which was very unusual in those days.

Like Aesop before him, and Rudyard Kipling after him, Leonardo liked to write short stories, typically with animals as the subjects, and a moral message as a conclusion. His fables and tales were often pointed, and often humorous.

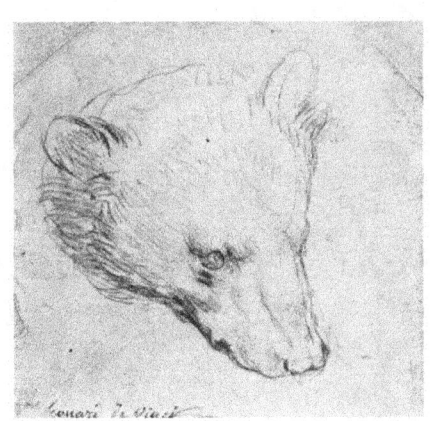

One of his many fables:

"A rat was besieged in his little dwelling by a weasel, which with unwearied vigilance awaited his surrender, while watching his imminent peril through a little hole. Meanwhile the cat came by and suddenly seized the weasel and forthwith devoured it. Then the rat offered up a sacrifice ... of some of his store of nuts, humbly thanking his providence, and came out of his hole to enjoy his lately lost liberty. But he was instantly deprived of it, together with his life, by the cruel claws and teeth of the lurking cat."[18]

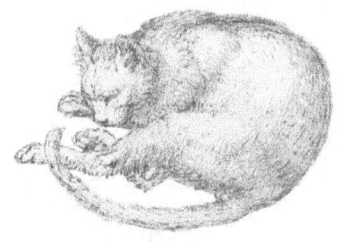

"The smallest feline is a masterpiece."

---

[18] *This fable is one of the 19 fables translated from Italian in The Notebooks of Leonardo da Vinci, Volume 1.*

Leonardo da Vinci and the Human Body

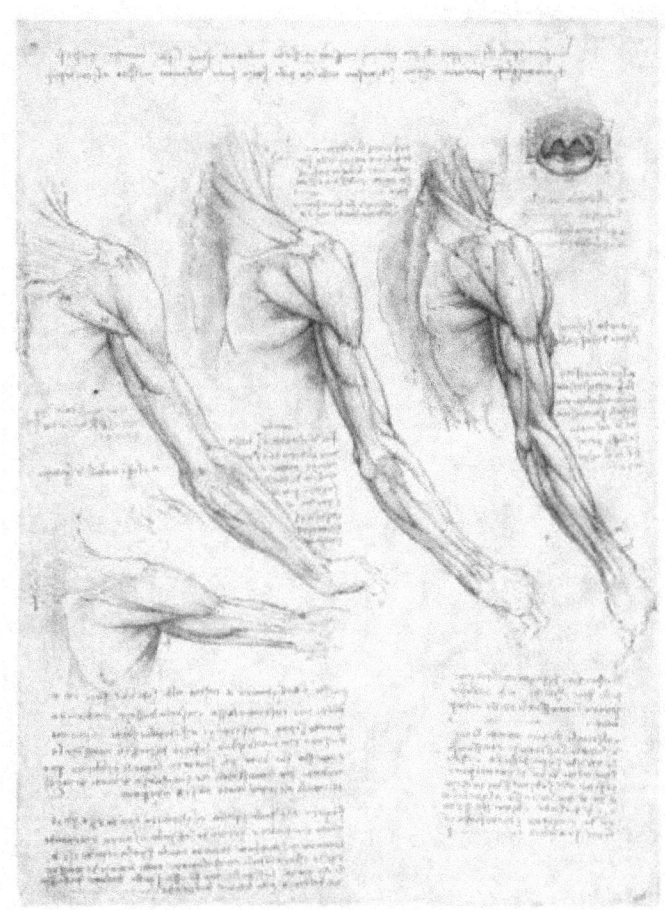

*"A wonderful instrument,
the invention of the supreme master."*

"The painter who is familiar with the nature of the sinews, muscles, and tendons, will know very well, in giving movement to a limb, how many and which sinews cause it."

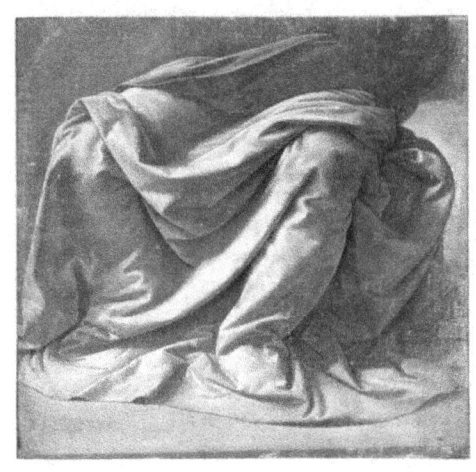

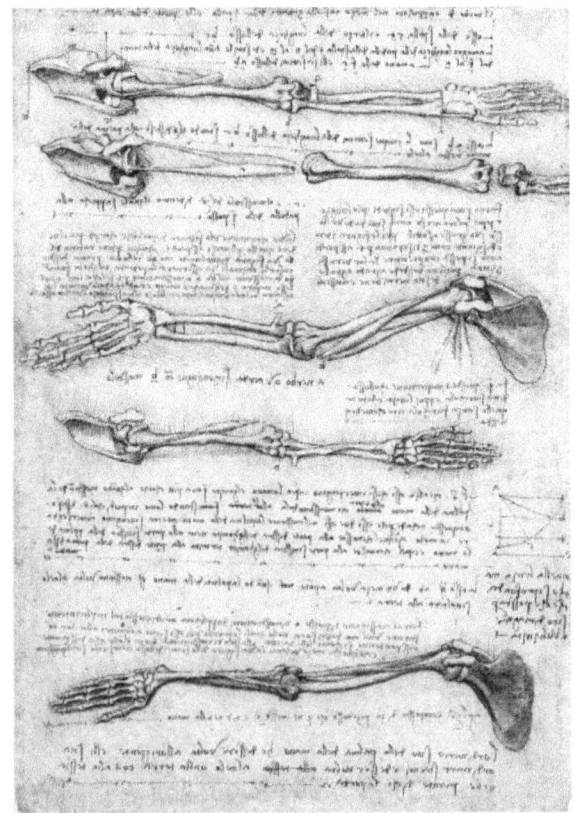

Student Activities:

We discussed da Vinci's dissection work, and his interest in anatomy as it helped him with his art.

Then we focused on his Vitruvian Man and the human proportions he observed. Splitting the class up into groups of two or three, we had the students measure each other to fill out the Human Proportions chart. Then we compared everyone's results, and discovered when da Vinci's predictions were accurate.

Leonardo da Vinci merged art and science throughout his life. His understanding of optics led him to improvements in shadows and perspective in painting, and his knowledge of geology and geography improved the quality of the landscapes he drew and painted. And his knowledge of anatomy improved the realism in the human figures he drew and painted.

Leonardo da Vinci was very interested in human anatomy because it allowed him to be a better painter. He wrote:

"The painter who is familiar with the nature of the sinews, muscles, and tendons, will know very well, in giving movement to a limb, how many and which sinews cause it."

His knowledge of anatomy improved the realism in the human figures he drew and painted.

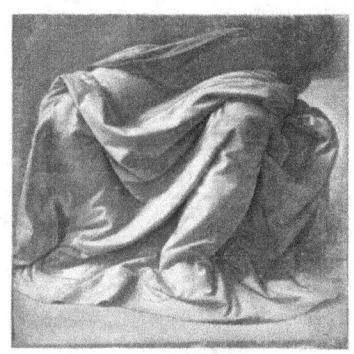

As he learned more about the human body, Leonardo wrote: *"A wonderful instrument, the invention of the supreme master."*

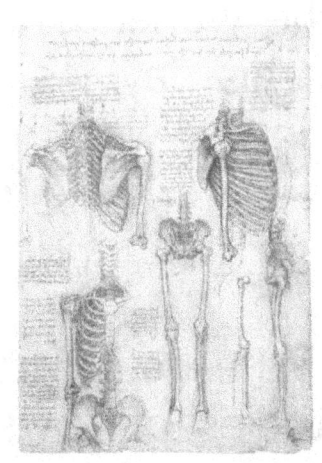

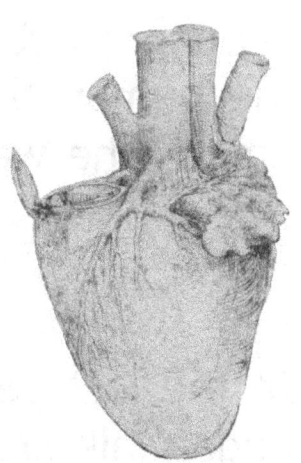

Leonardo's anatomical studies are among his greatest contributions to science. He is credited with being the first to make anatomical drawings in the manner still used today – using four sketches to show each part. He was the first to make cross-sectional drawings of the body showing veins, arteries, and nerves in this manner. He was the first to make anatomy studies truly a visual science, relying primarily on an abundance of pictures rather than words.

One of Leonardo's most incredible drawings is that of the "Embryo in the Womb." It takes my breath away to see something so "pro-life" that was drawn five hundred years ago!

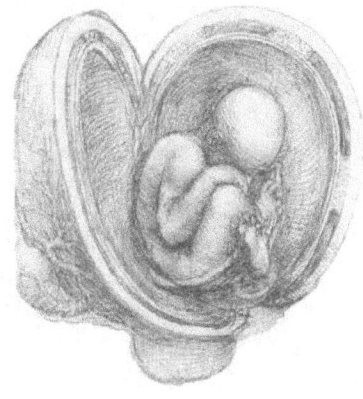

Leonardo actually knew more about the workings of the human body than most doctors in his day. As a painter, he was particularly interested in the way the eyes worked. To see was to perceive, was to be able to draw...

In the last years of his life he studied the heart. He began his study of the heart with studies of cows' hearts. He compared the flow of blood to the flow of water. And, of course, Leonardo studied the human skeletal system.

Leonardo drew his Vitruvian Man to show the "ideal proportions" of the human body. He based those proportions on his studies of the human body through the years, and the measurements he had taken. It was not an idea that originated with Leonardo – but once again he was the one who took it to a higher level.

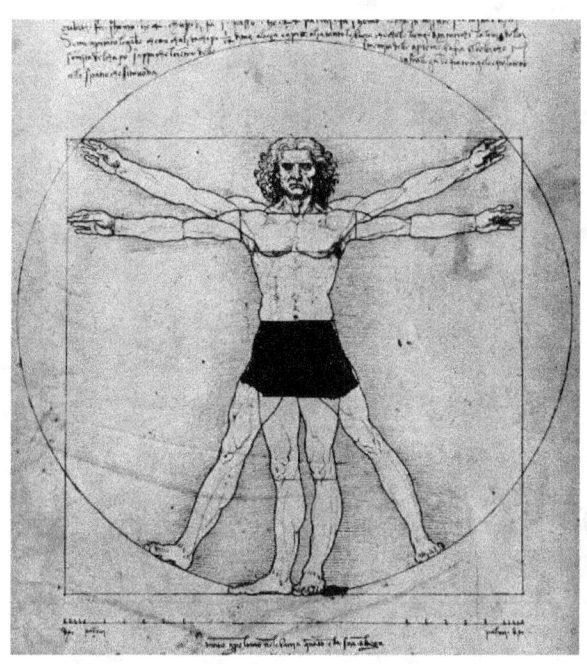

Leonardo da Vinci drew his "Vitruvian Man" to demonstrate the ideal proportions of the human body. Leonardo was not the first to come up with this idea – Vitruvius, a Roman architect and engineer 1400 years before Leonardo, had come up with similar measurements – Leonardo took it to the next "logical" step, and drew the man he was describing. The charts on the next two pages show some of the proportions Leonardo observed.

---

[19] *Of course, this picture is my "slightly edited" version of da Vinci's Vitruvian Man.*

HUMAN PROPORTIONS
ACCORDING TO DA VINCI

Some interesting observations, made by Leonardo of "similar proportions":

Between shoulder bones	Between hip bones		
Mouth to bottom of Chin	Big toe	1/6 of foot	
From wrist to elbow, and elbow to armpit (when arm is bent).		Length of one foot	
From the fissure (opening) of mouth, to the bottom of nose		1/7 of the face	

The mouth to the bottom of the chin	The mouth's length	1/4 of the face	
The end of the eye socket (towards the ear), to your ear	The length of the ear	1/3 of the face	The bottom of the chin, to bottom of the nose
Middle of the nose to the bottom of chin		1/2 of the face	
The eyebrows to the bottom of the chin		2/3 of the face	
Beginning of hair to the bottom of the chin	The hand	1/10 of height	

One hand	1/3 of the arm	1/9 of height	
Full head		1/8 of height	
The foot	Face	1/7 of height	
Top of the chest to the crown (top) of the head		1/6 of height	
Elbow to the wrist		1/5 of height	
The max width of the shoulders	Sole of foot to lower edge of knee	1/4 of height	Top of head to middle of chest
Arms out full length		Full height	

While the similarities he "discovered" don't hold true on each individual person, we found them to be close in a surprising number of cases.

Your Measurements Compared to Leonardo's Predictions[20]

Explanation: Measure the body section listed in each section of chart. Calculate each of the fractions shown (3/4 Height, 1/2 Face, etc.)

Compare – do the measurements in each section equal the calculated ones Leonardo predicted? (Typically, some do, and some don't.)

---

[20] *For your family or class*

Measurements in inches or centimeters	Name	Name	Name	Name
Height				
= Arm span				
Kneeling				
= 3/4 Height				
Elbow to Wrist				
= 1/5 Height				
Foot				
= Face				
= 1/7 Height				
Middle of nose to bottom of chin				
= 1/2 Face				
Mouth to bottom of chin				
= 1/4 Face				

Leonardo da Vinci was in Rome from 1514 to 1516. He had hoped to join Michelangelo and Raphael doing great artwork for the Pope, the head of the Roman Catholic Church, but his reputation of not completing projects had preceded him, and the Pope wasn't interested in hiring him. Leonardo did more of his scientific work in those years in Rome. He also traveled to Pavia, Bologna, and Milan during this time.

In 1515, the new French King, Francis I, traveled into northern Italy to prove his strength against those in that area. While in Italy, he met Leonardo da Vinci and invited him to France.

Several other artists were living and working in Rome at the time, and Donato Bramante was building St. Peters Cathedral. But, apparently Leonardo had little contact with them at this time, and may have been quite lonely at this period of his life. This may have contributed to his acceptance of a job in France.

Leonardo built a mechanical lion in 1515 for the celebrations in conjunction with Francis I's coronation as King of France. The lion was capable of movement and when it opened its mouth, it revealed lilies. Leonardo's lion was written about in other contemporary accounts, not just his own.

Leonardo's Occupations

R	M	M	G	N	U	Q	D	D	Q	W	F	V	B	H	K	J
I	U	Y	I	G	A	S	Y	A	O	A	I	T	N	F	L	K
L	S	W	I	L	H	I	R	I	P	U	F	G	Z	O	X	I
N	I	X	D	A	I	C	C	P	T	M	X	S	X	S	L	J
I	C	N	C	M	H	T	R	I	V	N	R	I	A	C	V	I
V	I	L	Z	I	W	E	A	N	T	R	G	C	W	U	T	H
K	A	E	T	C	N	F	D	R	I	A	U	C	V	L	N	Z
R	N	E	H	T	G	A	T	T	Y	N	M	I	B	J	F	Z
O	C	O	I	C	X	N	V	L	S	A	V	E	N	E	S	E
T	K	C	Y	R	Q	A	C	I	S	I	D	E	H	B	Z	V
P	E	H	G	U	O	T	C	G	A	A	T	V	N	T	Y	A
L	C	C	B	B	I	O	U	W	R	T	U	N	I	T	A	M
U	K	F	R	T	H	M	R	T	C	C	I	S	E	S	O	M
C	H	V	M	U	Q	Y	I	L	R	H	Z	O	X	I	O	R
S	A	I	A	Q	P	S	R	E	E	N	I	G	N	E	C	R
Q	H	Q	Q	O	T	O	A	F	B	T	Q	Z	B	W	C	S

1. Musician	7. Artist
2. Aviation	8. Mathematician
3. Scientist	9. Architect
4. Anatomy	10. Sculptor
5. Engineer	11. Apprentice
6. Inventor	12. Military Advisor

A Sample
of Leonardo Quotes

"Man is the model of the world."

"He who thinks little errs much."

"Learning never exhausts the mind."

"Art is never finished, only abandoned."

"There are three classes of people: those
who see; those who see when they
are shown; those who do not see."

"The noblest pleasure is the joy of understanding."

"The human foot is a masterpiece
of engineering and a work of art."

"I have been impressed with the urgency of doing.
Knowing is not enough; we must apply.
Being willing is not enough we must do."

A BRIEF LOOK AT
LEONARDO DA VINCI'S LIFE

Dates:	Events in Leonardo's Life:
1452	Leonardo is born at <u>Anchiano</u>, two miles from <u>Vinci</u>.
c.1455	Leonardo moves to <u>Vinci</u> to live with his Grandparents.
c.1466	Moves to <u>Florence</u> with his father to apprentice with Andrea Verrocchio.
1472	Leonardo paints angel in Verrocchio's *Baptism of Christ*.
1473	Leonardo makes his Landscape Drawing, his oldest surviving drawing.
1480	Leonardo works for Duke Lorenzo de Medici, a patron of the arts.
1481	Commissioned for *Adoration of the Magi*, his first large painting.
1482	Leonardo offers service as engineer and architect to Duke of Milan.
1483	Moves to <u>Milan</u>; contracted for first *Virgin of the Rocks*, that he doesn't finish; starts initial sketches for the equestrian statue for Duke of Milan.
1488	First Anatomical drawings appear in his notebooks.

1490	Leonardo directs pageants; makes scale model for equestrian statue.
1493	Builds full-scale clay model of the horse statue, unveiled for wedding.
1495	Begins *Last Supper* in the dining room at the Santa Maria delle Grazie.
1497	Leonardo illustrates Pacioli's new geometry book, *On Divine Proportion*.
1498	Leonardo makes plans to publish his notebooks.
1499	Leonardo's clay horse is destroyed by French soldiers invading Milan.
1500	Makes his way back to <u>Florence</u> where he begins work on *Madonna and Child with St Anne*. *The Last Supper* mural is already deteriorating.
1502	Leonardo serves as military engineer and cartographer to Cesare Borgia; traveling with throughout <u>Romagna</u>. Leonardo designs a bridge.
1503	Returns to <u>Florence</u> to great honors. Commissioned for painting of *Battle of Anghiari*; begins *Mona Lisa* (working intermittently on both).
1505	Finishes full-size sketch of *Battle* painting; does many nature sketches.

1506	Stops work on his *Battle* painting; finishes the *Mona Lisa*.
1508	Returns to <u>Milan</u>, where he is employed by French King Louis XII, currently living there; he begins major anatomical research.
1513	Leonardo goes to <u>Rome</u>, at request of Pope Leo X's brother, Giuliano. He opens art studio but concentrates on his science work.
1515	Constructs mechanical lion for Francis I's coronation. Paints last known picture: *St John the Baptist*.
1516	Leonardo moves to <u>Amboise, France</u> to work for King Francis I as "Premier Painter and Engineer and Architect." He dies on May 2nd.

Important Places in Leonardo's Life

S	I	G	P	Z	M	H	E	H	L	T	B	Z	U	X	L	X
A	O	B	G	I	H	S	R	L	V	I	R	W	O	X	E	E
Q	X	T	O	R	T	L	T	Z	I	L	L	M	V	K	I	H
F	E	J	T	S	L	A	L	Y	N	J	X	A	W	J	D	X
E	S	P	F	O	P	L	L	S	C	K	F	M	N	X	R	P
A	Z	P	T	V	M	H	C	Y	E	B	R	D	O	J	V	G
H	E	Y	R	X	W	A	O	F	Y	I	A	F	O	X	N	E
O	B	G	C	L	Y	F	N	R	V	S	N	V	P	V	N	C
K	C	O	Q	I	V	K	H	E	U	B	C	Y	J	V	L	N
U	X	C	E	E	H	R	Q	U	M	S	E	M	O	R	Y	E
M	X	A	M	B	O	I	S	E	A	P	S	G	V	H	Z	R
K	L	P	U	Q	V	I	C	S	B	K	I	T	R	Q	N	O
A	N	C	H	I	A	N	O	T	T	M	C	R	R	T	Y	L
V	P	A	A	Z	I	S	O	T	B	Q	Y	N	E	A	C	F
V	T	G	S	N	B	E	U	F	K	E	S	U	T	B	I	M
J	R	P	C	Y	Z	A	G	N	J	R	E	N	N	A	T	T

1.	Bosphorus Strait	5.	Rome
2.	France	6.	Italy
3.	Florence	7.	Ottoman Empire
4.	Anchiano	8.	Amboise

(1452 – 1519)

- Johannes Gutenberg (1398-1468) – inventor of the Western printing press
- Pope Alexander VI, born "Rodrigo Borgia" (1431 – 1503)
- Andrea Verrocchio (1435 – 1488) – Italian artist, musician, goldsmith
- Pope Julius II, born "Giulano della Rovere" (1443 – 1513)
- Donato Bramante (1444 – 1514) – Italian architect
- Luca Pacioli (1445 – 1514) – Italian mathematician
- Christopher Columbus (1451 – 1506) – Italian/Spanish explorer
- King Henry VII (1457 – 1509) – King of England
- Maximilian I (1459 – 1519) – Holy Roman Emperor
- King Louis XII (1462 – 1515) – King of France, cousin of King Charles VII
- Desiderius Erasmus (1466-1536) – Dutch reformer
- Niccolo Machiavelli (1469 –1527) – Italian political thinker, author of The Prince
- King Charles VIII (1470 – 1498) – King of France
- Albrecht Durer (1471-1528) – German painter, scholar, and author

- Nicolaus Copernicus (1473-1543) – Polish astronomer
- (Buonarroti) Michelangelo (1475-1564) – Italian artist
- Pope Leo X, born "Giovanni de Medici" (1475 – 1521)
- Cesare Borgia (1475 – 1507) – notorious Italian military dictator
- Sir Thomas More (1478-1535) English statesman, wrote Utopia, wouldn't recognize King Henry VIII as head of church in England (movie about them: Man for All Seasons)
- Ferdinand Magellan (1480 – 1521) – Portuguese explorer
- Raphael, born "Raffaello Sanzio" (1483-1520) – another great Italian artist
- Martin Luther (1483-1546) "Father" of the Protestant Reformation
- Hernando Cortez (1485 – 1547) Spanish explorer of the New World
- Titian, born "Tiziano Vecellio" (1477-1576) – Italian artist
- King Henry VIII, King of England (1491 – 1547)
- King Francis I, King of France (1494 – 1547)
- Charles, grandson of Ferdinand and Isabella (1500 – 1558) – ruled as Charles I of Spain, beginning in

1516, and Charles V, Holy Roman Emperor, beginning in 1519.
- Giorgio Vasari (1511 – 1574) Italian artist and author of *Lives of the Artists*

Other noteworthy folks who lived soon after him included:
- Tycho Brahe (1546-1601) – Danish astronomer
- William Shakespeare (1564-1616) – English author
- Galileo (1564-1642) – Italian scientist

www.ingramcontent.com/pod-product-compliance
Lightning Source LLC
Chambersburg PA
CBHW081130170526
45165CB00008B/2617

* 9 7 8 1 4 5 6 5 7 7 1 1 7 *